WAKE UP, SLEEPING BEAUTY

ALSO BY JANE ADAMS

Sex and the Single Parent
Women on Top: Success Passages and Personal Growth
Making Good: Conversations with Successful Men
Tradeoffs
How to Sell What You Write
Good Intentions
Seattle Green

WAKE UP, SLEEPING BEAUTY

How to Live Happily Ever After—
Starting Right Now

JANE ADAMS

WILLIAM MORROW AND COMPANY, INC. • NEW YORK

Excerpt from *Hers: Through Women's Eyes*, by Erica Abeel, edited by Nancy Newhouse, copyright © 1985. Reprinted by permission of Villard Books, a division of Random House, Inc.

Excerpt from *Through the Flower* by Judy Chicago, copyright © 1975, published by Doubleday Books, a division of Bantam, Doubleday, Dell Publishing Group, Inc.

Excerpt from *Four Quartets* by T. S. Eliot, copyright © 1943 renewed 1971 by Esmé Valerie Eliot. Reprinted by permission of Harcourt Brace Jovanovich, Inc.

Excerpt from "A Real Life Fairy Tale," by Lisa Grunwald, copyright © 1988. Reprinted by permission of *Esquire*.

Excerpt from *About Men*, by Edward Klein and Don Erickson, copyright © 1987. Reprinted by permission of Pocket Books, a division of Simon & Schuster.

Excerpt from "Toward a New Definition of Singleness," by Rachel Kranz, copyright © 1986 and published in *Sojourner*. Reprinted by permission of *Utne Reader*.

Excerpt from *The Seven Laws of Money*, by Michael Phillips, copyright © 1974. Reprinted by permission of Word Wheel Books, a division of Random House, Inc.

Excerpt from *The Working Woman Success Book*, by *Working Woman* editors, copyright © 1981. Reprinted by permission of Ace Books, a division of Berkeley Publishing Group.

Portions of Chapter 8 have previously appeared in *Working Woman*, of Chapter 9 in *New Woman*.

Recognizing the importance of preserving what has been written, it is the policy of William Morrow and Company, Inc., and its imprints and affiliates to have the books it publishes printed on acid-free paper, and we exert our best efforts to that end.

Library of Congress Cataloging-in-Publication Data

Adams, Jane.
Wake up Sleeping Beauty : how to live happily ever after—starting right now / Jane Adams.
p.   cm.
ISBN 0-688-08754-X
1. Single women—Psychology.   2. Self-actualization (Psychology)
I. Title.
HQ800.2.A33   1990
155.6'33—dc20   89-49710
                                                                 CIP

Printed in the United States of America

First Edition

1 2 3 4 5 6 7 8 9 10

BOOK DESIGN BY STEPHANIE BART HORVATH

To Sally, with gratitude and affection

ACKNOWLEDGMENTS

I would like to thank the experts who offered their time and knowledge: Dr. Ned Hallowell, Dr. Richard Soderstrom, Marvin Thomas, ACSW, Dr. Pepper Schwartz, and Dr. Jane Mattes. Their professional wisdom was invaluable in writing this book.

Additionally, I am grateful, as always, to my many friends who shared their lives, support, and wisdom; their contributions are acknowledged, even if, in some instances, their real names are not.

Contents

Contents

Contents

Introduction

IS THIS BOOK FOR YOU?
This book is for you if:

- You're a single woman who never expected to stay that way.
- You've been divorced so long you've forgotten there are worse things in life than being alone.
- Your biological clock is running down and you still don't have a child.
- You're a single mother who wonders if you're shortchanging your kids by not providing them with a man.
- You've put off important life decisions in case a man comes along to change them.
- You've delayed buying a house, a fur coat, or a piece of serious jewelry because a man is supposed to buy those things for you.
- You've been meaning to start a retirement plan, but you haven't gotten around to it yet.
- You dread birthdays, holidays, Sundays, and most of all, New Year's Eve.
- You're still saving Paris for your honeymoon.
- You never really made a choice between a career and a family; it just happened that way.
- You worry about who will take care of you if you get sick.
- You've stopped accepting invitations from married friends or going to baby showers.
- You can't remember the last time you woke up next to someone you loved more than two mornings in a row.

- You think that by not marrying, you've let your mother down.
- You wake up in the middle of the night wondering if you'll be lonely all your life.
- You feel like everyone else belongs to somebody but you.

WHAT THIS BOOK ISN'T ABOUT

This book isn't about why you haven't found Someone to Love and what you can do about it. It doesn't suggest that you plumb your psychological depths to learn why you keep attracting the wrong kind of man or what you find dull about the right kind. It doesn't assume that if you'd just redesign your body, your soul, or your expectations you'd never be lonely again.

This book isn't for you if you're still wringing your hands over That Study—the one that says it's easier for a smart woman to get a MacArthur genius award than a husband, or that someone with her own Gold Card, a peppy personality, and not one inch of cellulite on her body has a better chance of being hijacked by a terrorist than being swept away by a man with the right stuff.

This book isn't for you if you're considering moving to Alaska because the man–woman ratio is better there . . . if you've been in therapy for ten years and still aren't sure if you're sending the wrong messages to the right men . . . if you belong to a support group for Women Who Read Too Much.

ARE YOU READY TO GET ON WITH YOUR LIFE?

This book is for you if you're ready to stop postponing your life and start living it now. To start believing that you can experience passion, richness, excitement, intimacy, joy, and purpose as a single, independent woman who may very likely remain that way.

This book is for you if you're ready to start living in the present instead of the past or future. If you're not sure you want a mate but think you want a child. If you could use a community of loving, caring friends. If you'd rather your career feed your life instead of eating it. If you know that a meaningful existence comes from what you give, not just what you get. If you think it's possible to love yourself even though the right man doesn't. If you're ready to take yourself off hold.

I've been a single woman for over half of my adult life. When I think back now over the number of years I spent waiting to be defined by someone or something else, I think of the story of Sleeping Beauty.

Everyone knows that fairy tales are for children. Those were the myths that lulled us to sleep when we were very young, and even though as adults we may have forgotten some of the details—can you name all seven dwarfs? remember what the frog prince retrieved from the pond? identify King Thrushbeard?— their essence has not yet escaped us. Engaged at that time in the child's task of creating the self, we absorbed those myths, internalized those fantasies. Seeping into our unconscious, they cast their spell on us. Because we were girls, we identified with the heroines or princesses of the tales—they were our earliest, and therefore strongest, role models.

Most of them waited, and most were ultimately rescued from actively taking responsibility for their own lives. The only one who went out and sought her destiny, Goldilocks, ended up alone in the forest. Beauty gave herself to a beast—that he turned out, in the end, to be her perfect lover was a nice touch, but as we all know, most beasts don't, they just get more beastly.

Sleeping Beauty is a myth that gave us a way to see ourselves when we were young girls. Its essential theme was passivity, and so we waited to be acted upon often long after it was useful, appropriate, or practical.

In the fairy tale, Briar Rose spent a hundred years waiting. And because it was a fairy tale, she hadn't changed a bit when she woke up. She still had her youthful beauty, her glowing prospects, and all the gifts the good fairies gave her: wit, wisdom, charm, beauty, warmth, compassion and an eighteen-inch waistline.

Today's Sleeping Beauties aren't comatose in a castle, but they might as well be. They're sleepwalking through their careers, rearranging their social lives in case a man calls at the last minute, looking at bag ladies in the street and wondering if they'll end up that way. They worry that when their parents die they'll have no one to lean on at the funeral. They're enrolling in classes on how to find happiness through the personals, looking for meaning in crystals, gurus, or Gucci briefcases, and seeking maturity in all the symbols of adulthood: Will a mortgage do it? a promotion? a few gray hairs? But inside, they still feel like little girls, imprisoned in a thicket of thorns.

In the meantime, extraordinary things are happening in the world, but the Sleeping Beauties hardly notice. Great opportunities are passing them by every minute, while they still wait for someone or something to rescue them. It might be a prince. It might be a purpose for living. It might be the moment when the spell of eternal adolescence is finally broken, and true adulthood is magically bestowed upon them.

This book is for you if you're waiting, too. For a man—the husband, lover, life partner who still hasn't shown up, and maybe never will. For meaning—for an answer to those existential questions you last asked yourself ages ago—who am I, where am I going, what's it all about? For maturity—that indefinable something you'd expect to *feel* as well as *be* by now; at home in the world, connected, sure, and secure.

Like the princess in the fairy tale, and like many women I know, at or around the time my culture and my hormones indicated it was time to get married, I fell into a deep swoon. When I awakened, I thought, something would have happened. A man would have fought his way through the thorns and thickets of singles' bars, therapists' couches, and a zillion other clutchy, desperate women to find me. And when he kissed me into life I'd live happily ever after.

He did, but we didn't. So I waited some more. First for another man, who would magically rescue me from real life. Then for something else to claim me, some purpose more exalted than earning a living or fulfilling other people's expectations of what and who I should be. And then for something besides another birthday to convince me that I was, at last, a grownup. I was continuing, as Jung expressed it, to live an experience for which I had not yet found a name.

It's surprising how even those of us who are old enough to know better often believe that both meaning and maturity derive from a man. It shouldn't be, though—that's the myth we've been raised on. So often when women recount the dreams they had when they were little, they can never remember what happened after the last strains of Lohengrin faded in their fantasies. After that, it was all a blur, a blank screen like the one you see when the lights go up after the movie is over.

Remember the Life List you made when you were eighteen? It was full of things you promised yourself you'd do someday. Travel through Africa. Sing with a rock and roll band. Sky dive. Write a novel. Go to law school. Join the Peace Corps. Read Proust in French. Make a fortune. Start your own business. Build a house. Make a difference in the world.

Have you done any of them yet? Why not?

Now think about the Wish List you used to have ... not experiences, but things you wanted way back when. Pure silk lingerie. An exciting job. A leather coat. Diamonds. A house with a garden. A white leather couch. A stock portfolio.

Do you have any of them yet? Why not?

Everyone's Life and Wish Lists are different. Every list reflects individual tastes and longings. Most of us blame the things we haven't accomplished or acquired on circumstances beyond our control—time, money, and opportunity. We can't afford six weeks in Africa so we settle for a weekend out of town. We're too old to join a rock and roll band so we sing in the shower. We can't fit law school into our schedule so we take a real estate class one night a week.

As for the things we always wanted that we have managed to get, we save them for Later. We don't light the special scented candles unless there's company for dinner. We use the good silver only on special occasions. We don't wear the silk underwear if there's no man to appreciate it.

I once helped a friend go through her mother's possessions after she died. Her mother's home was full of beautiful things she was saving for Later: a hand-stitched silk nightgown that had never been worn, an unopened bottle of Joy, a set of Irish linens still in its original wrapping.

Why are you putting life off?

Have your fantasies faded a little every year, your sense of possibility dwindled into a vague feeling of dissatisfaction—despite the reasonable, legitimate explanations you give yourself for why you've let the things you wanted to do and to have slip away?

What are you waiting for?

Or have you let their importance fade because you believe, way down deep in your heart of hearts, that none of the things on your Lists can compare in value, significance, or happiness to being perfectly loved by one perfect man?

How much longer are you going to wait?

Some Sleeping Beauties believe that, without a man, they don't exist yet. It's as if nothing that happens to them truly counts, and nothing will until they find their heart's desire. They believe that love and/or marriage will make everything better, and without it, nothing can really be wonderful. They believe Mr. Right can shield them from pain, disappointment, and discouragement, and that good friends, an interesting job, economic independence, a sense of humor, and thin thighs are nice to have, but not really necessary if you have a good relationship.

Many of these women are only existing *until*. Marking time *until*. Just getting by *until* the Prince arrives, and Real Life, fol-lowed by Happily Ever After, begins.

In the last twenty years I've watched a social, sexual, and dem-ographic revolution alter women's lives and change the ways we think, believe, and act. I've met women who married early, married late, and didn't marry at all. Women with good relationships, bad ones, serial and singular ones, and many with no relationships at all. Every one of us has dealt with the issue of being single, at this time and this place in history. We all went through a stage when the word *single* defined how we saw ourselves, and in so doing, limited our vision of what life had to offer us, and what we had to offer life. You will meet us in the pages that follow—you may already know us, or women like us. We have lessons to teach, wisdom to share, and practical, useful suggestions for clarifying values, figuring out what's really important, and getting it.

The one thing we won't tell you is that any or all of these strategies for successful living will help you find a mate. If they do, and if that's what you want, terrific. What they *will* do is make you so engaged in working, playing, learning, or doing that you'll have more on which to pin the hopes of a lifetime than a Prince who may never arrive. Because the reality is that he may not. That you may never find anyone you like well enough to spend a lifetime with. Or that by the time you do, you may have discovered that you'd just as soon be single.

This book is for Sleeping Beauties who have a lot more choices than they think they have. If you're one of them, wake up. You've been dreaming your life away, and it's time to start living it while you still can.

1

Taking Yourself Off Hold

In addressing this book to you, the reader, I'm making certain assumptions about you. That you're somewhere between twenty-five and plastic surgery. That you've had some education and work at a job that on a good day feels like a career, but sometimes seems like only a paycheck. That you're single now, although you may have been married, and even be raising a child or children alone. Somewhere in your past, and maybe your present, there's at least one relationship you think of with a capital "R." You can't pass up those magazine quizzes that analyze your personality in twenty questions or less, but you're old enough to know that nothing's that simple, not even when the answers *don't* contradict each other. You've read a few self-help books in your time, because it's cheaper than therapy—or because you've been in therapy, but aren't sure you asked the right questions. At least once in your life someone has told you that you're too smart for your own good—your mother, your best friend, your boyfriend, or your boss. And in your heart, you knew they were right.

However, despite everything you know, the answer to one particular question still eludes you: *What do you want to be when you grow up?*

No other question evokes greater anxiety in women. In the answer are all our selves, all our ages, all our histories, experiences, and expectations—the ones we cling to and those we've

19

given up. In the answer are our differences, and also our similarities, the distance we've traveled, and the distance yet to go.

We were asked that question the first time when we were very young. And most of us, then, said the same thing: "wife and mother." We may have enlarged our response later on—added a goal or definition consistent with our age, education, attainments, and role models. But part or all of our original vision of who we always thought we would be someday has endured, even if we've become too sophisticated to articulate it to anyone rude enough to ask. In fact, the more we've repressed or suppressed it, the more powerful a determinant of our behavior and attitude it has often been, no matter who or what else we've managed to achieve or become.

Even today, with hardly any pinnacle from Everest to the Oval Office inaccessible to women, that earliest goal often determines not only the shape and texture of a woman's life, but the degree of satisfaction she takes in her accomplishments and the extent to which she defines herself as successful.

Psychologist and Harvard professor Carol Gilligan has pointed out how central intimacy is to women's identity—that we not only define ourselves in a context of human relationship but also judge ourselves in terms of our ability to care.[1] Therefore, the absence of a caring relationship, which many of us still define as a husband, as we did when we were little girls, often robs us of the vision to conceive of other goals, the energy to achieve them, and the pleasure of fulfilling them.

That is not to say we don't set or achieve some if not all of our goals. But often, if we have no one to care for, those goals lose their urgency, flavor, and determination. And in our urgency to care for someone else, we neglect to care for ourselves. If, in our eagerness to merge into another, we neglect the responsibility of the self to the self, we will never fill that empty place deep inside that longs for coherence and connection, never awaken that Sleeping Beauty who has waited all these years, and is still waiting, for someone or something to give her life meaning.

Intimacy means close familiarity with and connectedness to; caring means noticing, attending, nourishing. Yet often the self we think we know is really a stranger, and the one we notice, cherish, and comfort is the child of long ago rather than the adult we have become.

Try this exercise. Make a list of three things you have, and three that you want. Is any of them sufficient to constitute a whole self? Probably not.

Now try this one. Write down everything you ever wanted to be, from the earliest time you can remember, and everything you remember ever wanting to have. Think about the goals you abandoned—why and when you did. Chances are you let go of those hopes and dreams because (a) you got them; (b) you didn't; or (c) you got something else instead.

Now look at what's left. Is there anything on that piece of paper you couldn't have or be—*if you were willing to give up everything else?*

Well, of course there is. You probably can't be a prima ballerina anymore, and it may be too late to be the first woman who (fill in the blank). But the real value of a list like this is illustrating that much of what mattered to you long ago has changed, just as you have.

What's important to you today has been modified by time and experience. Some illusions have been abandoned, and other limitations imposed by choice, chance, and age. But no one easily abandons any part of herself, especially not the essence of her earliest myths. No matter what you have achieved—a role, a possession, a career, a relationship—you may still be tending the child you were rather than attending to the woman you have become. Although by now you may have given up Sleeping Beauty's fantasies, you may still be trapped by her spell. You cannot loosen its hold on you until you grieve for the loss of those fantasies, confront your disappointment and sadness, let it be, and let it go. Until you do, you will not have the energy you need to live fully in the present with the woman you are today.

MYTH AND METAPHOR—OR, SLEEPING BEAUTY STARTS TO STIR

There are truths embedded in myth, and magic in stories. They can be powerful tools for helping us model or make sense of our lives. But first we must distinguish the one from the other—the truth from the magic. The truth of woman's nature is not that she is passive, but that she is receptive. But in the transmogrification of the Sleeping Beauty myth into the cultural role of women, the distinction has been blurred.

Passivity and receptivity are very different states. A psychiatrist, writer, and teacher, Charles Johnston, distinguishes them in a medical metaphor: "Passivity is a cellular inertness. It manifests either as tissue too rigid for impulses to penetrate or too flaccid to interface or significantly respond. Receptivity, on the other hand, is precisely a tissue's degree of excitability. It is a statement of vital responsiveness, of who we are as a unique meeting with our living existence. Receptivity is readiness to possibility."[2]

I was very excited when I read this. It was a distinction I'd been seeking for a long time. But I had problems with the image in the sentence that follows: "Receptivity is Sleeping Beauty at the moment of the Prince's kiss."

If that's true, too, what does it say about all the hours, days, and years before that moment occurs? And what if it never does? How does that suggest ways in which a single woman can fashion a life that is creative, generative, and satisfying? If we give up the fantasy Prince, do we also give up the possibility that he'll ever arrive? If we're out there beyond the walls of the castle, living with purpose, intention, and connection in a changing and unpredictable world, how will he know where to find us?

Perhaps we cannot erase the Sleeping Beauty myth from our unconscious. But we can replace the image of a passive adolescent with one of a receptive woman, break the rigid, impenetrable trance, and awaken to the possibilities that are all around us once we leave the castle.

As grown women, we need to wake up Sleeping Beauty, and

send her on her way. We must find other heroines to replace her, and other catalysts to transformation and empowerment besides Princes, Daddies, or Beasts. Today we need new ways to see ourselves, new myths and metaphors to explain who we are, to mediate between our unconscious longings and the selves we have or might develop.

Art and literature can guide us to new stories. So can our dreams, in which the unconscious resolves conflicts we may sense but not entirely understand. Meditation, intense physical exercise, changes in pattern or habit, a direct encounter with nature, a journey, however brief, to an unfamiliar place—whatever gets our mind *off* our mind—are other ways to unlock the imagination, find images, metaphors, or analogies to our state or condition, and create a different story from the one we've been telling ourselves all these years . . . a story in which we are the heroines, the agents of our own destiny, the woman who makes change happen, and, in the process, is changed herself.

Kate, who introduced me to scuba diving, used to say that the most transformative experience of her life was a sea change—literally as well as figuratively. The experience of diving offered a new metaphor for my existence, as it had for hers. Confronting the unknown, going beneath the surface, being weightless, freed of the constraints of gravity—the whole experience was rich in symbols that really spoke to my life. As Kate put it, "Every time I surface, my ideas about who I am and what I could be expand. I am powerful in a way I never imagined before."

Singing lessons helped Peggy find the voice that had been silenced in a repressive early environment where Southern girls were taught to be seen but never heard. "The first time the teacher told me to let it all out, this incredible *power* came pouring out of the deepest place in me! It was a voice I never knew I had. It didn't matter that it was untrained, off key, impure—it was just there, allowed at last to come out. It made me wonder what else was in there."

For Phyllis, a nun's costume which she donned one Halloween

became an outer symbol of an inner sense of invisibility. En route to the party, her car broke down: "I walked to the gas station, noticing how people responded to me, especially men. They glanced at the habit, and then they simply didn't see me. I didn't exist for them. It seemed right, fitting, congruent with my own feelings about myself. And that really pissed me off! When I took the costume off later that night I felt my power flow back into me—I felt *visible*, able to be seen. I began to act more assertively the next day. I began to ask for what I wanted—acknowledgment—at the office, with my friends. And my sense of what could happen in the rest of my life *if I were willing, if I insisted on being seen*, changed dramatically."

It's not coincidental that often the word "powerful" surfaces in stories and symbols of women discovering their hidden selves. For that is the aspect of our natures that often seems to close off the possibility of connection, that animus, as Jung calls it, in which resides our authenticity, our true self, the wellspring of our power to act autonomously and claim our identity. It seems so *unfeminine* when we feel it stir. We disown it because we think it threatens men (as it often may). But more often we ignore it because it threatens us, urges us to action, and demands that we take responsibility for our lives.

BEAUTY'S LONG SLEEP

Waiting is a time-honored part of women's lives. It begins in childhood, when everything wonderful seems to be scheduled for later. We sense very early that it is not our will, but the will of others, including Mother Nature, that defines the parameters of our life. Faith Wilding's poem, "Waiting," echoes our younger selves:

> Waiting for my breasts to develop
> Waiting to wear a bra
> Waiting to menstruate.
> . . . .

Waiting for life to begin, Waiting—
Waiting to be somebody.
. . . .
Waiting to get married
Waiting for my wedding day
Waiting for my wedding night.
. . . .
Waiting for the end of the day
Waiting for sleep. Waiting . . .[3]

The effect of this waiting metaphor is deep-seated and insidious. It contributes to our feeling that we are not in control of our lives. If it does not paralyze us entirely, it ensures that whatever we do manage to achieve by our own efforts will seem tainted, somehow, as if we achieved it by cheating or manipulating—or that the achievement is trivial or insignificant, compared to what a man might have bestowed on us—or inauthentic, because it is incongruent with what we imagine our real role, our true identity, to be.

And, most pernicious of all, Waiting keeps us from truly committing to anything that could not be easily gotten rid of if someone came along with a better offer. In an *Esquire* article about Diane Sawyer, Lisa Grunwald described the newswoman's home like this: "Her apartment was empty, a place for in-between things, and, perhaps, a place of waiting. If you are single and a woman and you spend too much time picking out fabrics and buying nice plates, it adds a certain permanence to your situation. Every purchase is an investment in a life you may still hope to jettison."[4]

This article, tellingly titled "A Real Life Fairy Tale," was about Sawyer's marriage, at forty-two, to Mike Nichols. "I still believe in lightning striking," she said, but it is clear from her accomplishments that that didn't keep her from living a great (if somewhat unfurnished) life until it did. Even Sawyer lost patience with all the friends who told her, before her wedding, how radiant and happy she seemed. "After all the work she'd done, all the days she'd dragged her body into the office and been a professional, to hear that she only seemed happy now smacked too much of 'All you needed was a good . . . man.' Maybe it was hard to be so happy, because it seemed to suggest that she hadn't been all right before."[5]

But happiness is a full house that always has room for more. Sawyer's life before she married Nichols illustrates that crucial difference between passivity and receptivity—and the only truth in the Sleeping Beauty myth that is meaningful to women today. Passivity is a dead-end street, but receptivity is the road to empowerment, to the possibility of embodying the "whole in one" who resides in all of us. Passivity goes nowhere, but receptivity leads to congruence, and congruence to connection.

What makes myths so compelling is the power they represent. In most myths, women do not exercise power—they respond to it. The metaphor that represents power may be a kiss, a magic mirror, a glass slipper, but it is always something which is conferred on a woman, not something she can get herself. When you rewrite the myths you live by, however, and create new metaphors that speak to the capable, adult woman you are today, something magical happens; you move the power to create the life you want from outside to inside of yourself.

THE MEANING OF MEANING

If myth is the bedtime story of the unconscious, and metaphor the symbolic key that opens the door to consciousness, context is the connection of each to the other—the shape, pattern, or fabric that determines meaning. When you live your life in the expectation of the Other, as fairy tale heroines do, whatever does not connect to him or fit into that fabric seems unimportant and valueless. Life is a series of unconnected events, a voyage with no destination, a journey without direction. It simply becomes something that happens while you're making other plans.

Self-actualization is one context in which many women play out their lives. As the excesses of the so-called "Me Decade" and the media-styled narcissism of the eighties illustrate, this can be, by itself, so narrow as to constitute a preoccupation with ego gratification and a callous disregard of the needs and rights of others if they conflict with one's own. Or, to paraphrase Fritz Perls, that consciousness guru of the human potential movement: You do your thing and I do mine, and if by chance they coincide, terrific, but if they don't, tough luck for you. But self-actualization can also be a context in which self-knowledge leads to true engagement with others, where your hopes of accomplishing your full potential to create and to love may be realized.

Rebellion is a context which appealed to many women who came of age in the heyday of the women's liberation movement. Overthrowing the old order, in which women were constricted by patriarchal attitudes and systems, became the guiding principle of many lives. For these women, engagement with one of the great social movements of our time enhanced and expanded their lives as well as the lives of others; they engendered both pride and possibility in all of us, though often at great personal cost to themselves. Many of "those who carried the torch," as poet Carolyn Kizer says, "got first-degree burns."

Janet, who was one of those torchbearers, said, "When I was a girl, I wanted to run off and join the circus. Instead, when I was a woman, I ran off to join the revolution and change the big world. It seems to me now that I might have been wiser to remain where I was, and try to make smaller, less dramatic changes in my own world. But I wouldn't have missed it—that sense of being caught up in a purpose larger than I was. While my life is now focused on the personal, the domestic, the Movement is the lens through which I view the world, and it shows me plenty of chances to make the small, undramatic challenges every single day. I try to act, as William James said, as if what I do makes a difference. And I believe that because I do, it does."

Freedom is another context that found expression in the sexual revolution two decades ago. The Pill freed many women from the prison of their own biology, and others from repressive attitudes that blocked full sexual expression, but, as some women learned, to their surprise and often their sorrow, sexual emancipation alone did not make them happier. Indeed, the cultural framework that transmits older values from one generation to another has been assaulted by social and technological change, fragmented by mobility, and distorted and exploited by the media and the marketeers. We are left in a vacuum, which may be one reason why old archetypes and stereotypes seem to be reappearing, why there has been such a swing back to some of the more repressive attitudes of the past about what women's proper role should be. While we have come too far to turn back, the current is no longer with us.

Drama is still another context familiar to many women. Crisis and conflict make us feel alive, alert; satisfaction with our lives and relationships bores us. And peace of mind continues to elude us, even as we seek it. In the resolution of one crisis, we sow the seeds of the next. Joss was happy only when there was tumult in her life—no job, man, or situation was stimulating enough to suit her. Every time she felt bored, she rearranged her life—she rid herself of one lover and took another, she discarded old goals and sought new ones. At every turn she looked outside rather than within herself to create the stage on which her life could unfold, with her at the center. And when the curtain fell, as it always did, there she was, alone on that stage, in the empty theater of her self, listening to the sound of one hand clapping.

What, then, is a suitable context for you—one that gives meaning to your actions, coherence to your goals, and relevance to your life? Where is the pattern in the things and people and ideas that please, provoke, and challenge you? In short, what is the purpose of getting up in the morning, and what are the accomplishments that let you sleep at night, secure in the knowledge that what filled your days had meaning?

BEA—A LIFE WITH PURPOSE
Bea and I ran into each other at a stoplight. From this smashing beginning came a friendship that has lasted for over a decade,

during which she has awed, inspired, and often aggravated me. Awed and inspired because she has accomplished so much—turned a few volunteers and a minuscule budget into a thriving community-based organization mobilized to treat and prevent AIDS. Aggravated because so often I've seen her exhausted, dispirited, overworked, and underpaid, unacknowledged, underrated, and exploited. Balance, says Bea, can wait for later. Right now, people are dying.

Yet even at the end of an eighteen-hour day, there is something unquenchable in Bea, some spirit that sustains her and makes her feel, most of the time, that regardless of how the war is going, her own personal struggle to leave the world a little better than she found it is a worthwhile one. Important enough to put her own needs second—Bea always needs a haircut, and she still hasn't finished the last few credits toward her degree, and her last relationship collapsed because of logistics—there just weren't enough hours in the day. It wasn't that her lover resented her commitment to her work—he had commitments of his own, a demanding job, a teenaged son, a spiritual practice that took up several hours every day and seemed to Bea very remote from her own life—inner-directed, while hers is focused somewhere else.

Bea worries, in the moments before she falls asleep at night, that her biological clock is running out. That she hasn't been to the gym in weeks. That it's been a long time since she's seen her closest friends. That one day she'll wake up and life will have passed her by. She saw a therapist for a while because she deals with death and dying every day and her own mortality felt shaky. "Are you happy?" I ask her from time to time, and she looks up at me from under her shaggy bangs and says, "Happy? Whoever said you're supposed to be happy?"

But yes, she admits, she is happy. "I'm making a difference," she says. The things her friends take for granted—comfortable surroundings, new cars, occasional vacations, a whole weekend to read, play, cook, make love, see movies, do laundry—are special to her. She's no martyr—she's simply very, very focused. She makes the free time she has count—she uses it to restore her energy, replenish her resources. "Nothing that really, really matters is missing from my life," she says. "The fact is, if I had been willing to put a relationship first—or even second—I would be in one now," she avers. "If and when I meet the right man, I don't think I'll have any trouble setting priorities. And that's true of all the essentials in my life. I get a little of most of the things I need." A little time, a little luxury, a little recreation, a little love. But does she get enough, I wonder? "Life is like money—there are two ways to look at it. Either you make more, or you make do with less," says Bea. She makes do with less because it gives more meaning to what she has. Sometimes she gets less comfort, but more satisfaction, out of things other women take for granted. She can make a vacation out of a Saturday away from the office. She savors every second of the time she spends with friends; when she's with you, she's really present, and if you need her, she's there for you. She's soft and blond and pretty, but her blue eyes aren't as starry as they were when she was younger and she thought she could change the world. Now she'd be satisfied if she could just make it better for some people who live in it. That isn't all of who Bea is, but it's a big part of her—the part that includes others, makes them want to give to her, connect to her, love her. There isn't a day that goes by whose passing she doesn't notice. There isn't one coming she doesn't have hope for.

This is what I learned from Bea: *A year from now, nothing will have happened except that a year will have passed—unless you make something else happen. Time, like life, doesn't care—it just passes.*

Enlightenment, commitment, a religious or spiritual center, a balanced life, success, self-respect, service, security, effectiveness, the advancement of political or social ideals, health, knowledge, awareness—any or all of these can constitute a context and suggest goals that support it.

Life has no meaning without a connection between the self and its external environment. A purposeful context is what takes your life off hold and makes you stop waiting for someone or something to give it meaning. It is the knowledge that what you do with your life matters, and that *that* is the meaning, the meaning that connects the inner journey and the outer event.

AUTONOMY AS A CONTEXT FOR YOUR LIFE

Autonomy is not possible for the woman who has put her life on hold while waiting for someone to appear and complete it. She may be financially self-sufficient, accountable to no one for her time, perfectly capable of functioning in the real world, and able to spend her resources as she sees fit, but she is not truly autonomous—not as long as she is in thrall to a fantasy Prince, or shopping for a guru in the spiritual supermarket, or looking outside herself for an identity, or assuming that someone else's ability to make right choices is superior to her own. Nor, very often, does she want to be. She has not recognized the value of autonomy, perhaps because it carries with it the sometimes frightening concomitant of responsibility. To herself, her career, her creativity. To her intimates, family, and friends. To whatever and whomever matters in her world.

The society that nurtured us has not, until relatively recently, construed autonomy as a worthwhile context for women. Autonomy last appealed to us just about the time we fell into Sleeping Beauty's long doze. Freed of the constraints of our parents' rules, expectations, and purse strings, we imagined then we could be anything or anyone we wanted to be. But when we woke up, what we wanted to be was Connected. Autonomy meant too many choices, and freedom, as Janis Joplin put it, was "just another word for nothing left to lose."

But what autonomy really means is freedom to choose the meaning of your life—what it will stand for. And often what keeps us from embracing it is the misperception that by joining our life to someone else's, we no longer need to take responsibility for how it turns out. *Autonomous* does not necessarily mean lonely, and *free* rarely means irresponsible. What autonomy does mean is that you are free to choose and pursue the principles, activities, and relationships that support you as a Primary Woman—economically self-sufficient, socially and emotionally independent, and responsible for your own happiness. The obligation of autonomy is that you must stand *for* something, *by* something, *in* something. And often you must do it alone.

Imagine what could happen if you rewrote the myth of Sleeping Beauty in the context of autonomy. Imagine a tale of the possible-you that begins this way:

"Sleeping Beauty tossed restlessly on her narrow cot. Sunlight woke her, and when it did, she looked at the perpetual calendar on her watch and noticed that she'd been asleep for years. So she decided to go out into the world and see what had changed during that time."

Endow Sleeping Beauty with all the characteristics you'd like to have: courage, intellect, curiosity, beauty, and charm. (You had them all before you fell asleep, remember.) And, just to make it interesting, give her those traits you recognize in yourself today: restlessness, dissatisfaction, loneliness, occasional churlishness, a trace of cynicism, a feeling of boredom that comes and goes. Pack Sleeping Beauty a bag containing whatever is essential to her life: a Daily Planner, a degree, talent, or skill that could support her during her journey, the phone number of a friend she can call if she really needs to, a map or a guidebook. (You don't have to know what it's a map or guidebook to—at least, not yet.)

And now pick up a pen and write. Forget that you have no imagination—you have. Don't worry about the fact that your heroine doesn't know where she's going—she'll end up somewhere. Just keep her eyes open. Make sure she notices the scenery along the way. Pay attention to the people she meets, and listen to what they tell her. Have her stop at a crossroads and decide on a direction. Describe what's going on inside her—her feelings, fears, and physical reactions. Have Sleeping Beauty come upon a barrier of some sort, and figure out how to get around it. Keep her going. There is only one rule to remember: Though she may dally with a Prince along the way, she cannot stay with him longer than overnight. If she does, she'll be back in the castle, imprisoned there again.

When you look over what you have written, you may be surprised at how the elements of your life appear, just as those tantalizing bits of dreams you remember on awakening correspond, but not quite, to the realities of your waking hours. They may seem cloudy or muddled at first, but if you look closely, you'll recognize them. Sleeping Beauty's barrier may be a raging river or a wicked witch, while yours is a fear of being out of control or fear of your mother's disapproval. Don't expect a line-by-line, literal correspondence between your story and your outer life—and don't try too hard to make your story logical. If logic were all, you wouldn't need to start with a story—you could go right to the real thing, your life, and change it in a second.

2

Too Smart for Your Own Good

A little self-knowledge can be a dangerous thing. It can lock us into ways of being, believing, and behaving that inhibit our potential to transform our lives, as it has for Linda.

Linda left academia one thesis short of a Ph.D. and found a job in industry. By now she's well up the career ladder. She's acquired a great apartment, a lavish wardrobe, matches from Manhattan's best restaurants, a sophistication that gives no hint of the chubby, pageboyed "grind" she was in high school, and a repertoire of stories in which she is always sadder but wiser afterward, stories that end with that mocking, ironic, vaguely bitter chuckle that carries the silent message, Don't you dare feel sorry for me.

Linda has never been in therapy, but she knows herself very well. She believes that intelligent people can solve their own problems, and that no one should expect to be happy all the time. She is a great analyst of her own life: She can remember the exact moment she internalized the message that she wasn't pretty, that men are dumb, that people can't be trusted, that love doesn't last. She knows precisely when she learned it wasn't OK to be who she was, that people who had authority in her life—her parents, her teachers, her friends, her lovers—would like her better if she were someone else; clever but not too intelligent, sexual but not demanding, alive but not quite so lively, good but not excellent.

But all that self-knowledge has become, as Linda gets older and more cynical, is a barrier to feeling. Linda is good at keeping life at a distance. Her cynicism is a carapace that protects her like a turtle's shell. In small doses it's funny, but after a while, it tints everything gray, like a cloud that blots out the sunshine. On the way home from a lunch with Linda, I sometimes want to pick up a child and hug it, or jump into bed with a man—commit some life-affirming act that will reconnect me with hope instead of despair.

In Linda's life, as in everyone's, there are moments when meaning is made; events that carry a message or emotion forward in time, so that what really occurred fades in memory while what remains is exactly how it felt when someone fell short of your expectations, injured your pride or your ego, dashed your illusions, or discounted your vulnerability. And when something happens today that stimulates those same feelings, the part of you that psychologists call the subconscious or the observing ego makes the connection between then and now—even if, on the surface at least, there is none.

That is the aspect of herself that Linda knows best. Yet it is only one aspect of Linda. There are at least two more, as there are in all of us. In every human being there are permanent, varying, and multiple states of consciousness, fluctuating levels of awareness. While we function primarily in one state or another, our mind is constantly at work, shifting back and forth among the others, even if we're not aware of it. Psychologists and philosophers have assigned different names to these aspects of self, and it gives me a headache to remember which is which. So, following is a three-dimensional metaphor to use when considering them. Within each dimension, each state of consciousness, are the symbols that help me understand them. Yours may be another metaphor, other symbols, but these are the ones I'll use throughout this book when I talk about the aspects of self that can keep Sleeping Beauties imprisoned in their castles or awaken them to the possibilities of a world beyond the walls.

SMALL MIND, BIG MIND, GREAT MIND

The aspect of herself that Linda knows best, the one that determines how she thinks, feels, and acts, is what I call Small Mind. Small Mind is the way you interpret what happens to you, the meaning you've made of all your experience, and the personality, character, and behavior that have resulted. It is what makes you eager or frightened, trusting or wary, critical or supportive, disciplined or casual, competent or ineffectual, hopeful or pessimistic, intuitive or rational. It's whatever an analytic woman like Linda can consciously, if hazily, recall learning, seeing, hearing, or feeling that she knows had an influence on her. It's the answers you give to all those "what type are you?" quizzes, the things you tell a shrink or therapist in the first few hours. It's the self you're most conscious of, your first level of awareness; how solid or permeable it is depends on how old you are, how often you reflect on how you think, feel, and act, even how many self-help books you've read. It's the position you take on you.

Small Mind's job is sorting. It is constantly reinterpreting present experience on the basis of the past, making new experience congruent with old feeling. Small Mind strives for connection—important when what you need to remember is how it felt when you burned your fingers on a hot stove so you won't do it again, but counterproductive in many other situations. Small Mind insists that since you were hurt, disappointed, or injured the last time, you'll be hurt, disappointed, or injured this time, too. And while Small Mind is connecting *then* with *now*, it's also formatting the future, laying both experiences down on Sleeping Beauty's grid.

Small Mind can keep a Sleeping Beauty living in the past or future—in the past, when something hurt her and in the future, when something else might. Like Linda, Sleeping Beauty may be aware enough to remember those moments when meaning was made; and, like Linda, she may have great intellectual insight, but be unwilling to reconnect emotionally with those moments. Not unconsciously, as Small Mind does when it relates then to now and floods us with a feeling from the past, but consciously, with our adult awareness of all the layers of experience since then, all the aftershocks that reinforced that original meaning. Small Mind is so resistant to change that, in order to do so, we must do more than recall a feeling or experience—we must, literally, re-member, reconfigure what we know by combining it with other, sometimes contradictory information.

How each of us views the world depends on the power and focus of the individual lens, and the way that lens was first ground, as writer Judith Guest says; the feel of absolute permanence about it is what makes change so difficult.[1] Sometimes the help of a good therapist is necessary. But sometimes we can mitigate Small Mind's influence by acknowledging and understanding the other levels of consciousness that are always available to us.

I think of Small Mind as a room filled with files. I can read the labels on some of them: Early Toilet Training, Hot Stove, Boys Are Stupid, Math Block. Other labels are obscured by dust. There are several files that have no labels at all. The file folder my mind dredges up at any given moment is often directly related to my current preoccupation; at other times I really have to ponder it to understand the connection, especially when the labels read: You Can't Do That, There'll Never Be Enough, and my perennial favorite, Boys Like Girls Who Bunt, something I internalized back in sixth grade, when David Carlson ignored the fact that I had hit a home run off a softball he pitched, and walked Vicki Bonelli home from school instead of me.

Big Mind is another state of consciousness, that aspect of self which is constituted by the gender, culture, history, environment, even religious ideas, impressions, and imperatives that shaped you. It's composed of rules, role expectations, boundaries, obligations, and definitions that depend on who you are, how you were raised, what your culture and milieu told you about who you should be, and what might be possible in your life. How accessible to this level of awareness you are may depend on the degree to which you feel connected, or not, to your normative traditions, conscious of how being of a certain gender, class, heritage, society, and generation contributes to your view of the world and of yourself.

From these influences—or from your acceptance of or rebellion against them—derive your personal morality and value system. When Big Mind is particularly accessible it can provide an ethical, spiritual, or political blueprint for living. When it conflicts with Small Mind—when there is dissonance between what you think and what you feel to be true—you are likely to experience anxiety. This is the confusion that results when emotions are repressed or denied. But only when you open the door to this level of awareness, and think *about* your beliefs rather than *with* them, can you resolve that conflict.

One way to tap Big Mind is to make a list of descriptors that are appropriate for you. Here's one I found in the Personals section of an upscale newspaper: "Single WASP educated professional woman, not a Yuppie but still a few years away from the Big Chill, heterosexual, Scorpio, feminist, wants to meet someone with similar background to make love and babies in a nuclear-free world." While this woman may act and feel in ways dictated by Small Mind, her self-definition and her goals come from Big Mind.

Perhaps the greatest influence on Big Mind is gender. Since most psychological models are defined by a male perspective, much of what women know about themselves stems from deficit thinking. By that I mean a perspective, like Freud's, that focuses on what is absent, deficient, or wrong with us and assumes that we react to what is missing in ourselves. Sleeping Beauties often accept this perspective, reject their own authority and project it, in an idealized version, onto men. The more remote their authority, the more intense their yearning becomes for someone who can embody it for them, and the more apt they are to wait for him to endow it rather than call it up within themselves.

My image of Big Mind is a closet. In it are the clothes appropriate for all the roles I inhabit, now and in the past. The dress I wore to my confirmation. The graduation cap and gown. The siren outfit, the wedding dress, the maternity smock, the power suit, the flannel nightgown, and the silken lingerie. Sometimes all I see in the closet are shoes—patent-leather Mary Janes, sneakers, open-toe wedgies, sturdy hiking boots, my first pair of high heels.

Great Mind is what Jung calls the collective unconscious, the archetypes and metaphors whose understanding can lead to a deep sense of connection with the universe. Most of us are not usually aware of this level of consciousness unless we attend to it. Often it operates so far below the surface we only make contact with it in dreams, if then. We respond to it at an elemental rather than analytic level, in flashes of perception or recognition that seem to disappear as mysteriously as they came. It is often stimulated by sensory or aesthetic experience—sometimes it is a feeling of profound joy, or deep sadness, or brilliant clarity, or awe. Women often feel it in nature, experience it as a bond of connection with all of life, or in the pull of the moon that regulates not only the tides of the ocean but the life forces of menstruation, procreation, and lactation that wax and wane within us.

In Great Mind, too, there is that part of us that is, or longs for reunion with, whatever we recognize as divine; it is what my friend Marilyn means when she talks of the Intelligence that shows her the meaning. This level of Great Mind is as distant as the Andromeda galaxy to some, as close as a heartbeat to others. Often the only time we think about it, feel close to or disconnected from it, is when we consider death, and what, if anything, lies beyond.

For me, Great Mind is an undersea cavern, a place of mystery, creativity, and power. For the goddess Persephone this is the underground to which she descended. For Sleeping Beauty, this is the castle where she sleeps and dreams . . . and, perhaps, awakens.

OPENING THE DOORS TO PERCEPTION
Awareness does not occur in only one state of mind at any one moment. Our thoughts, emotions, beliefs, and behavior result

from the interaction of Small, Big, and Great Minds, a process that takes place without our realizing it, that feeds data from the external world into the inner one and determines how we think, feel, know, and believe, that shapes our perspective on self and others. In order to shift that perspective, we have to take control of the process.

Imagine that all the states of your consciousness are accessible. Imagine an Open Mind, with all the doors to your innermost self unlocked. You can animate this image if you try. Blow the dust off a file and riffle through its pages. What do you see there that you've forgotten? What's in there that's still influencing how you think and feel today? What was the moment when meaning was made? Is it still valid? Is this a message that still makes sense? Who put this in here, anyway—your father? your first lover? your fifth-grade teacher?

Then use your psychic energy to blow open the other doors to perception. To Big Mind, where all your roles and identities are symbolized by the clothes in your closet. To Great Mind, where creativity, generativity, and nature reside, and where the answer to the riddle of why you are here may be, too.

To move forward, you have to go backward, through the doors to perception. And understand that, as T. S. Eliot said:

> What we call the beginning is often the end
> And to make an end is to make a beginning.
> The end is where we start from.
>
> . . .
>
> And the end of all our exploring
> Will be to arrive where we started
> And know the place for the first time.[2]

IF YOU REALLY WANTED TO, YOU COULD

The doors to perception serve necessary functions. They keep us from being so overwhelmed with emotion that we are powerless to think, so inundated with the past that we have trouble staying with and responding to what is going on in the moment. They guard us from pain. They stifle anger. They create congruence, or at least its illusion.

To become more fully ourselves, however, we need to open those doors. To live wholly in the present, we need the energy stored in the past. Once it is in the present, we can harness it, put it to use in our lives. But we cannot always be sure it will go where we direct it. It may—it probably will—have a mind of its own, animate painful feelings and memories. To cope with the pain, we may resort to denial, escape, compromise, rebellion. But only by confronting ourselves honestly, participating fully in our feelings, can we transform them. And when we do, we are led to a new insight which has the power to transcend them, as Julie has discovered.

JULIE—GETTING BETTER, NOT BITTER

"I can't remake myself or you—I can only accept or relate to us both."

This is the aphorism that Julie has needlepointed on a pillow that occupies a prominent place in whatever dressing room she currently occupies. Julie is an actress, a woman who began in improvisational comedy clubs to discover herself. In her thirty-two years, she has freed herself of most of the constraints of her early life. She was orphaned when she was six, and in the series of foster homes that housed her for the next twelve years she was subject to various religious, cultural, and moral systems. "I adapted," says Julie. "That's the way I survived. But I never felt that any of those roles fit me. I wanted to be Someone, but I was never sure who it would be. Acting was like trying other Someones on."

So perhaps it was no surprise that Julie gravitated to the stage, that the alter egos she created for her comedy routines and, later, the roles she played in the theater, gave her both insight and practice in "looking at myself and the world through other people's glasses." To act successfully, Julie believes, you have to be in two places at once—thoroughly inside your character's head, "believing what she believes, feeling what she feels, while at the same time maintaining that part of you that's separate, detached, objective." That separate self, says Julie, employs and controls the actor's craft, uses its voice and body and mannerisms to create an illusion knowingly. "If there are no boundaries, you fall through yourself, into a place where you're lost, a place you can't get back from," Julie says. "I know that some actors don't feel this way—they believe in total immersion in a character. But that's never worked for me, perhaps because holding onto that piece of me, that core self, is what kept me alive all those years in all those places with all those people who wanted to mold me into their ideal kid. I need to know that when the curtain falls, I come home to myself, in the deepest sense of the word."

When she plays or creates a role, Julie starts from outside and works her way in. "I begin with the behavior, the words, the dialogue. When I did *Sister Mary Ignatius Explains It All For You* in a regional theater, I called on two years I spent in a Catholic school in Texas. It only took two days to get my lines down cold. I knew the system of belief that created this girl, because for a while I *was* her—after my folks were killed and I desperately needed something to cling to, to believe my parents were in heaven, safe in God's mercy. When I went deeper into the character, I could relate to how that particular system shaped her, and also how it failed her. The more clearly I saw it, the more I understood how those two years, those formative years that I spent in that environment shaped me, and how, even though I never became a Catholic, some of the ideas I now hold resulted from that exposure. And I saw how the title character could never have become anything different from who she was, either. I was able to dredge up compassion for her, see the moment when she might have acted differently, and understood why she didn't."

In that particular role, it was easy for Julie to create the life history the playwright implies for the character. In others, it has not been. "When I played the ingenue in *All About Eve*, in a revival I did two years ago, it was like putting on clothes that don't fit. It just went against all my conditioning to be that ruthless, that ambitious. Yet I could relate to having felt those emotions stifled in me as a young girl, being told that wasn't OK, wasn't womanly. As rehearsals went on, I began to understand and claim my personal ambition in a way I never could before. I could see what my character could see, what was holding her back, what weapons and strategies she could employ to get what she wanted. They weren't the ones I'd choose, but I could understand why she did. I think that role really changed me."

Some of the characters Julie creates for her comedy routines are "a way to understand who certain people are, and share that understanding with the audience. Or maybe it's about understanding parts of myself, real or fantasy selves. I have this one woman who is just walking liberation dogma. She interprets every single thing that happens to her in terms of oppression, being held down, the male-chauvinist world. She's a caricature—she calls men penocrats—but there's truth in her—there has to be truth. And I have another, a Superwoman who's got a househusband at home. He's the one who's making it possible for her to have it all, but the problem is that she's just not turned on by him. In assuming her roles, he's become feminized in her eyes. The guys in the audience laugh but some of the women cry. And when I'm him, that character, I feel just as trapped by society's expectations of men as I do when I'm Wilma, the women's libber."

Acting and creating her own characters, says Julie, "forces me to reexamine all my assumptions, all of the time, and find underneath them, the real person I am . . . not just find myself, but accept myself. The more I accept, the more I am able to open up to the negatives; the more I feel my limits expanding, the more compassion I have, and the more energy to create a wiser, more loving, less cynical self. There is a lot of bitterness in me for the tragedy that happened when my folks died. I've had to create a feeling of home—a place where someone will always take you in and love you. That place is in my heart, and I guess that someone is me."

Wake Up, Sleeping Beauty

This is what I learned from Julie: *Insight confers power, and that power can help us change. In that power is choice—the ability to make new decisions about how we will act; compassion—the capacity to forgive ourselves; connectedness—the state in which we are a part of all living things; and congruence—the authentic self we seek.*

❧ 3 ❧

A Life for Yourself

The myth of Sleeping Beauty is not the only childhood fairy tale that influences how we experience ourselves as women. In the story of Goldilocks, we learn that solitude is synonymous with loneliness and that seeking our destiny outside of relatedness leads into the dark forest of separation. Yet the truth is that it steers us toward autonomy, in which we can value solitude as well as cherish intimacy.

As girls, we learned very early to define ourselves in terms of our relationship to others; separation anxiety is bred in us when young. And so, as adults, we acknowledge our need for intimacy, but give short shrift to solitude, as if it is nothing more than what's left in the wine glass after the party's over.

Solitude is a child's habit lost in a busy grownup world. Children are often preoccupied with the workings of their own mind—thinking, learning, creating, imagining. This process of self-discovery gives way to the discovery of others; ultimately, the world calls out to us, and we answer. Some of us never recover that inner contentment with our own presence; others do, and wonder if our desire for it means we are immature, frightened of intimacy, or unable to love.

"Am I being selfish? Withdrawn? An introvert? Does being my own best friend mean I don't need others?" asks Hallie, a happily single thirty-three-year-old who worries that she's *too* happy.

"Maybe that means I'm unfit to really love somebody, or even live with another person. But I have always preferred solitude to a lot of company. Sometimes I have to force myself out."

In Hallie's job as a social worker, she is constantly called on to meet the needs of others. Many other women in the helping professions feel the same way that she does and are just as concerned about it. "I worry that I'm pushing people away on the private side of my life, because I have this intense need just to be alone," says Nell, who works in a hospice. "You know what Heaven would be?" asks Clare, the principal of a metropolitan high school. "Heaven would be being married—but only from Friday to Sunday. If I didn't have evenings alone, at least during the week, I'd go nuts. Make that Saturday to Sunday. Like, starting around Saturday night."

According to psychiatrist Roderick Gorney, as women, we have been overfed and overstimulated on a diet of intense emotional relationships. This idealization of attachment and consequent devaluation of solitude has been absorbed into Big Mind, which reflects our cultural norms. But if we open our minds to other levels of awareness, tap into other aspects of the self, we can change our experience of solitude. In Great Mind, we can have access to imagination, intuition, and creativity, and feel an inner contentment with our own presence. In that part of us—Small Mind—that links unconnected events engendering the same feelings, we can feel a harmony and coherence remarkably similar to what we experience when we are intimate with another.

A number of vastly different events can trigger feelings of intimacy, and most, with the possible exception of sexual love, can be done in solitude. The self experiences them the same way, and so, if you allow it, can you. When you link solitude to self-discovery, to awareness of your deepest needs and impulses, it takes on a whole new coloration.

Solitude is not the same as loneliness, which has a toneless quality. According to psychiatrist Robert Weiss, the self associated with the absence of loneliness is a different one from the self associated with loneliness; it is more engaged by a range of interests, more confident, more secure, more self-satisfied. The lonely self, by contrast, is "tense, restless, unable to concentrate, driven."[1]

It is that self associated with the absence of loneliness, who, whether in privacy and seclusion or simply alone in a crowd, is the solitary being. To be successful and satisfied while alone is an acquired taste, like an appreciation of caviar.

THE USES OF SOLITUDE

We are socially conditioned to believe that any experience is enriched by sharing it; yet some of life's most sublime experiences—learning, creating, integrating, meditating, fantasizing, visualizing, dreaming, intuiting, transcending, and transforming—not to mention eating fettuccine with your fingers—can only be accomplished alone. But for every woman who treasures solitude, there are Sleeping Beauties who feel that unless they are connecting with others, they are invisible—it's as if they don't really exist. "It's the 'I Relate, Therefore I Am' response," says my friend Cookie, who makes up book titles like that in her spare time, and even, occasionally, in her job in publishing. (She'd like you to know she had nothing to do with this book's title, by the way.)

Sleeping Beauties can remake their attitude toward solitude, and thus their experience of it, suggests Barbara, who is too close a friend to be my shrink but often drops a pearl or two of professional wisdom *en passant*. She suggests one technique therapists call introjecting a good object. Basically, it means thinking of someone, real or symbolic, and moving that person or entity into your mind. With practice, you can call up that loving friend—sometimes just closing your eyes and picturing him/her in your head can do it.

Introjection is often a strictly unconscious process that's going on whether we're trying or not: When we wonder what so-and-so would do, say, or think about something, that's what we're doing.

Introjection may not be pleasant if that person in our head is a critic, judge, demanding parent, or other authority figure, so when you do this exercise consciously, make sure you're introjecting someone whose compassion, affection, and understanding you can count on, rather than someone whose love or respect is conditional on your behavior.

"The soul selects its own society/ Then shuts the door," wrote Emily Dickinson. Her poem offers a metaphor that can help you invite someone into your thoughts whose presence in your life fills you with happiness, populate solitude with a "good object." When I do this, I picture myself preparing for company, and dressing, putting my house in order—sometimes I can even hear the chime that signals the arrival of my "guest." And then I open a window, or a door, and usher my company in. Sometimes I do it physically, sometimes only in my mind, but either way, once that person is securely nestled in the easy chair of my consciousness, I feel centered, relaxed, and receptive to discovery and creativity.

Once I was describing this fantasy to my friend Carol, who was raised in a Jewish home where the lighting of Sabbath candles was a regular Friday evening ceremony until her grandmother's death. "After Bube died, Fridays were just like other nights—my mother put away the candlesticks, and we never did it again. There was something about that ritual that was very special for me—when Bube said the blessings and asked God to join us, I really felt Him come in. I imagined that the flickering of the candles was His breath, and for a few minutes I felt enfolded by this incredible, all-encompassing love."

Carol does not consider herself a religious person and has never since experienced that sense of God's presence. Yet she retrieved the Sabbath candlesticks from her mother's attic, and they occupy a special place in her home today. She lights them now "whenever I feel that particular kind of emptiness that, for me, means lonely." She does it not to bring God into her heart, but her grandmother, whom she remembers as "the only person in my entire life I felt wholly adored me, without reservation, not because of anything I did, but because of who I was—me, Carol."

When you begin thinking of solitude as a gift rather than a curse, you may develop your own fantasies or rituals to usher it in. Or you may depend on some kind of activity that will ring the doorbell for you, allow your mind to quiet so that whoever or whatever needs your attention can find it. Whether it is meditating, sorting the laundry, cleaning out your desk, or engaging in some solitary physical activity like running or swimming, it will lead you to that state where thoughts, feelings, and ideas interact and recombine with new meaning and insight; where even though the only change that has taken place has occurred within you, you experience the outer world in a very different, immensely more positive way.

When you are being a Sleeping Beauty who chooses solitude because people have failed you, because it is preferable to assuming responsibility for your own actions, or because it seems like the only safe place in a dangerous and frightening world, you create the alienating experience you will have in it. When you view it as a time out with yourself, a place to recharge your batteries and refocus your attention on the person who matters most—you—you will find it an entirely different, even compelling, environment. To develop, realize, and recognize yourself, you need only your imagination, which can bridge your inner and outer worlds.

HOW TO WIN AT DOUBLE SOLITAIRE

If intense relationships with others have been overvalued as important to happiness, then interests, skills, and even hobbies that can be pursued alone have been relegated to less than secondary importance. But they play an important role in defining who you are, and give meaning to your life as much, if not more, than relationships, which are what you bring the self *into*, not what is *created* by them. People who are passionately involved in pursuing interests cultivated over time can be quite happy even if they have only a few close relationships with others. By that I don't mean that love and companionship aren't necessary—they are. They provide recognition, acknowledgment, and affirmation; what other interests do is create and establish the you that they see, know, and approve. But if you demand that your interests give you something you want from others rather than help you incorporate a sense of your own value as a person, you will set yourself up for false rather than authentic satisfaction, because it will depend on the interest or approval of someone else. He can't give your life meaning—only you can.

Interests, hobbies, personal passions can all be vehicles for personal growth, just like relationships. Their changing nature and increasing maturity parallel our own, and they can lead, if not always to intimacy, at least to recognition and affirmation. That isn't to say that relationships make it impossible to pursue activities and hobbies that matter to you; in fact, some people choose some kinds of alliances for that very freedom, while others want intimacy for its intrinsic value. Often Sleeping Beauties believe that the most creative part of themselves comes alive in a relationship, and wait for someone else to stimulate it. But this is simply not true. No one can stimulate what isn't there to begin with—you can water a rock, but it will still be a rock. So ask yourself this: What part of *you* are you waiting for someone to animate? Your mind? Your body? Your intellect? Your social or political consciousness? You can choose to develop any or all of these by yourself . . . for yourself. And on the way to doing so, you will likely find others who are doing the same thing. But all they can be are companions on a journey you have chosen. When the search for someone or something to give your life meaning determines all your choices, you have no choices. The search is not a context for your life, nor should it be. If it is, you are living life lopsidedly.

Getting what you want for yourself rather than waiting for

someone to give it to you begins by using the resources you have right now for opportunities for achievement and happiness.

Many women I know choose their interests according to the opportunities they provide for meeting men. That's the advice we've been given since we first started reading *Seventeen,* and I blame it for a great deal: a broken ankle suffered in pursuit of the summit of a mountain I had no business climbing; a political campaign spent licking envelopes on behalf of a candidate I didn't care about; membership in half a dozen organizations ranging from a computer club to Save the Whales; and a sports car that spent more time in the shop than in my own garage. That advice made me steer clear of groups where women outnumbered men by a hefty margin and ignore the personal interests that either required solitude or weren't likely to lead to a lasting relationship, or even a date. When the activity in question involved a lot of men, I discovered, I focused on them instead of it; worse, I avoided anything that might involve competition, the possibility of looking awkward or foolish, or a leadership role. Yet when the activity was pursued for its own sake, not for a man, I experienced none of this avoidance, and whatever trepidations I suffered had to do only with my own safety, comfort, or abilities.

Of course, if the things that interest you also interest the kind of men who appeal to you (and you look good in the clothes they require), go ahead and take *Seventeen's* advice. Just be conscious of the fact that that, by itself, is not enough to sustain your interest, and think about the ways in which it may inhibit your full participation in any particular hobby or pursuit.

USE IT OR LOSE IT

The mind, body, and even the spirit can be avenues to discovering the interests that might engage the Sleeping Beauty in you who's trying to wake up. The ones that most fully capture your attention will nourish at least one and possibly all of these. They may interest or attract other people, but if they don't, that is no reason to cross them off your list. They will invariably lead you to other interests, and, if you want them to, other people.

THE WISDOM OF THE BODY

Waking up a Sleeping Beauty can be easy compared to getting her off the couch. For years I used the same excuse when well-meaning friends tried to interest me in anything remotely physical in nature. "I don't do anything that can't be done in three-inch heels," I said. "I'm a cerebral person, you know." Athletics generally meant muscle strain, gyms were places where everyone looked better than I did in leotards, and games were an arena in which I was likely to make a fool of myself.

My body was telling me, in a number of ways, that it felt let down. But I never let it help me feel better emotionally, either. It wasn't until I began to connect mental with physical well-being—to make the mind/body connection—that I was able to make a commitment to swimming or running on a daily basis. When I saw the link between spiritual growth and testing the limits of my body, as I did when I took up scuba diving, I found the perfect sport for me. When I stuck with a diet for a long time, not because I wanted to be thinner but because life had hit me with a number of low blows and I felt out of control, I learned how taking control of one tiny thing—what I put into my mouth every day—made it easier to deal with the others that were beyond my efforts. And when I tuned into Small Mind's message from my childhood about not competing with men, and Big Mind's gender cues about physical strength being a male prerogative, I understood why I'd been on the sidelines for years. And I started playing competitive games again—in all-women's leagues at first, and later, with mixed teams.

It's only in the recent past that I've come to understand that exercise is one of those things whose reward, generally, comes after instead of during . . . all those endorphins coursing through your body, making you feel alive, euphoric, and vital. Of course, exercise has other rewards, too, especially a well-tuned body. Just be aware that if your only reason for a well-tuned body is to satisfy some Other's fantasy of how you should look, you may not stay with it over the long haul.

THE DELIGHTS OF THE MIND

The brain is a marvelous thing. It's like a huge playground, and if you let yourself fool around in it, it can lead you out of yourself into a realm populated with others, both real and imagined. I'm reminded of a line from Woody Allen's *Purple Rose of Cairo*, in which Mia Farrow says to the actor who steps out of the movie and into her life, "I have a wonderful life, a marvelous relationship . . . of course, it's all fictional." What happens to her off-screen isn't nearly as fulfilling as her fantasy—yet what goes on there is real, too, as real as the life of the mind can be.

"When I was a child, it seemed that something—school, chores, meals—was always interrupting the real life I lived in books. Maybe because my mother constantly admonished me to get my nose out of a book and go outside to play, I grew up with a compromised message about reading: While it was encouraged and approved of, I always had the sense that it wasn't really as valuable as more extroverted pursuits involving other people or more active ones that exercised something besides my mind. My college roommate couldn't believe that I'd rather spend Saturday night with a good book instead of a bad date."

Go ahead—try to imagine the woman who said those words. You can see her now—a sallow, pasty-faced bookworm, shy, passive, with glasses as thick as her ankles, right? Wrong. Gloria is a stunning, outgoing thirty-five-year-old who worries that "there isn't enough time in my life to learn everything I want to know, especially the things I don't know anything about yet." Her tastes are eclectic, her friends varied, her interests wide-ranging— "everything I do, I first read about in a book." If something piques her interest, she reads up on it before she attempts it—"I've found that knowledge reduces fear to manageable proportions," she said just before she departed for a six-month trip around the world—alone. She said it again when she signed up for flying lessons. And again when she rewired her house. And once more when she decided it was time she understood computers. I once asked Gloria if she read for knowledge or entertainment, and she looked at me strangely: "Aren't they the same thing?" she asked.

Theories about information-overload notwithstanding, the brain is wondrously expandable; every bit of knowledge rearranges what you already know, changes your perspective, increases the possibilities of connecting with an interest, hobby, or pursuit that will expand not only your mind, but also your self-awareness, and add to your reservoirs of mastery and pleasure. There is no human endeavor that cannot be enriched by knowledge, no preference, instinct, sensory, aesthetic, or relational experience that can't take on added and perhaps undreamed of dimensions by putting your mind as well as your body behind it.

TRAVELS IN THE SPIRIT WORLD

The mind and spirit are not the same, although to many people they are synonymous. If the mind is the door to coherence, the spirit is the place where it is felt and integrated. I use spirit in a nonreligious sense here, to refer to a vital, natural force that animates both mind and body. M. Scott Peck, a psychiatrist who authored one of the era's best-selling books, *The Road Less Traveled,* makes no distinction between the mind and the spirit, and "therefore, no distinction between the process of achieving spiritual growth and mental growth. They are one and the same."[2]

It is clear from the increasingly spiritual aspect of many therapeutic approaches—for example, human potential, New Age, and transformational paradigms—that many people who once thought it necessary to choose between religion and personal growth are looking for a system of values and beliefs that can accommodate them both; a system that tends toward promoting a sense of coherence and connection rather than alienation, a means of linking what they recognize as mind and spirit, or knowledge and faith.

Many people engaged in a search for self-fulfillment or self-healing find that at its outer, or inner, limits, they encounter the divine in Great Mind. Others do not. My friend Dru, who has been engaged in that quest for some time, in and out of established religion, growth programs, and New Age movements, says, "The trick is not getting the right answers, it's asking the right questions." This is true, she says, whether the quest is self-directed or guided by a particular philosophy. "Healing or awareness takes place when you are ready to be healed or to be aware. When you're fully awake and ready to go on the journey, you find whatever guide is at hand."

THE DOUBLE BIND OF THE SINGLE LIFE
When you lead life for yourself, you have the option of inviting others to share it. When you lead it for others, you don't. The truly independent woman keeps her options open.

Men are culturally cued to value independence. It is that cue that gives rise to what Daniel Levinson et al. in *Seasons of a Man's Life,* termed the dream. "The dream is a young man's conception of what he might be in the adult world, a vision that creates excitement and the sense of possibility. A man without a dream of his own or a man whose life strayed too far from his dream could lose the sense of vitality that makes the adult years a time of growth."[3]

Because dependence has cued women's dreams, it has limited excitement and possibility to an Other. But if independence—not from others, but of and from the limitations of being a woman in a primarily androcentric society—were your cue, what kind of dream might it engender? What kind of excitement—what kind of possibility?

KIRSTEN'S DREAM—A LIFE WORTH LOVING
Imagine yourself as an adolescent girl living in a culture that did not expect or even allow you to marry until quite late in life—say,

fifty. Nothing else would be forbidden—not sexuality, not intimacy, not even having a child. How would that affect the choices you made about the thirty adult years you spent as a single woman?

"What a delicious fantasy!" said Kirsten. "First of all, I'd choose a career that was more open-ended than teaching life science to seventh graders, although I might come back to that much later. I think I'd have more to bring to my students then, having lived a fuller life, learned and experienced more. I'd get a different kind of education. I'd use college as a sampler, a way of trying out a lot of things that interested me, and when I found something that did, I'd get as much training as I needed to prepare for it, even if it meant, say, ten years in medical school . . . when you talk about a job that has to last a lifetime, it's worth it. I'd do something that could really make a difference in people's lives, in a big way if possible—after all, I'd have thirty years to accomplish it. I'd probably do a lot of traveling. If I decided I wanted to go to Paris for the weekend, and I had the money, I'd go. I'd plan my time to suit me, and I wouldn't have to explain where I'd been or what I'd been doing to anyone. I'd choose people to be my friends because I liked them, not because my husband did or didn't. I'd spend a certain amount of time alone, pursuing my own interests, thinking my own thoughts. I'd let the laundry pile up until I ran out of clothes. I'd eat crackers in bed and have dinner at midnight if I wanted to. I'd even get fat if I felt like it—if you don't get into the marriage market until fifty, physical beauty isn't such a big deal. I'd never wear high heels! If a relationship was making me crazy, I'd get out of it—*phfft*, like that, no lawyers, no hassles. I'd act out more of my sexual fantasies, but I'd spread them out a little more, not feel like I had to do everything fast, before I got tied down to one monogamous relationship. I'd probably have a child, maybe in my mid-thirties, so by the time I got married I'd have raised it according to my principles, not someone else's. There would probably be plenty of women and maybe even some men doing the same thing, so I'd have a community of other people to help me out, and they'd have me. There would probably be better public day-care programs, too, in a society like that, so that would help. But if I didn't want to have a child, there wouldn't be any pressure to . . . what a relief that would be. I think I'd take more chances. I'd probably move somewhere else—I've always wanted to live on the West Coast. If I got totally involved in something that was important to me, I could put my whole self into it without worrying about shortchanging a partner. By the time I got married, if I ever did, I'd have enough money, so that wouldn't be a factor in choosing a mate. If the marriage didn't work, I wouldn't stick around just for financial reasons—there would have to be more keeping me in it than that. And if I wasn't happy, I'd have no one but me to blame."

To me, the most interesting thing about this fantasy was that it came alive in the imagination of a thirty-eight-year-old woman who's been single all her life. It illustrates how much expectation has to do with outcome, especially the last sentence, which sums up what I learned from Kirsten: *If you're not happy, you have nobody but yourself to blame.*

There's nothing stopping Kirsten from living out that fantasy, because she already is independent—she just doesn't feel that way. She feels frustrated—by her age, her job, her boyfriend, her income, the demands on her time and energy. But frustrated is not the same as persecuted, which is something Kirsten is just beginning to understand. Several months after Kirsten shared her fantasy with me, she called. "Guess what?" she said. "I quit my job. I cashed in my teacher's retirement fund, borrowed some money, and I'm going to medical school! Want to have lunch?" Med school wasn't a given yet, but on the basis of her test scores and recommendations, she was hopeful. "That fantasy we did that day stayed with me—I just couldn't get it out of my mind. I went through all the 'what ifs'—what if I fail, what if my lover leaves, what if I'm making a huge mistake, what if I hate it? But there's something about just doing it—just taking your power into your own hands, realizing you really don't have to satisfy anyone except yourself, and being willing to make a lot of little compromises just to make that one thing happen. Like, Gary really isn't crazy about this whole idea. I think we may split up, as a matter of fact. And since I can't afford to stay in the house alone, I'll have to get a roommate. On the other hand, if we do break up, I could go to school somewhere else—I've applied in Oregon and Washington as well as to the three schools around here. And if I get in, and it's not for me, or I can't make it—well, at least I'll have tried. My dad said, 'At least you'll have teaching to fall back on,' and I looked at him and said, 'I'm not falling back on anything or anyone. If I fall, I'll fall ahead! And you know what? I'll have no one to blame but myself!' "

Sleeping Beauties' lives are full of "what ifs?" What if I lose this job and can't get another one? What if my father dies and I have to take care of my mother? What if my lover never gets around to making a commitment? What if I actually have to support myself for the rest of my life? What if my best friend moves away? What if I never have a child?

Autonomous, independent women ask themselves "what if" just as often as Sleeping Beauties do. "You just don't dwell on it as much," Kirsten said. "Not if you're where you want to be, doing what you want to do, or at least trying." Being where you want to be, found the authors of *Lifeprints*, a highly regarded study on patterns of love and work among women, is the major component of both mastery and pleasure, which make up well being. As such it determines whether the advantages of the single life feel right to the particular woman.[4] Being single was not Kirsten's major problem, "although I think I tended to blame whatever dissatisfaction I felt in my life on that. But being single and having a low-status, dead-end job—that was a real double bind."

When singlehood feels like a transitional rather than a stable state, Sleeping Beauties can get strangled by double binds like Kirsten's. Think about how you'd do things differently if you looked at the way you live now as a stable life structure, not a temporary, shaky situation, a way station on the way to maturity If your own life were your purpose, you'd invest in a career without worrying that it might disturb your relationship or even make you "too masculine" and therefore less marriageable. You'd have a child if you truly wanted to, if you chose that avenue to connection with the future as well as the past and present. You'd live exactly where and how you chose. You'd be a competent manager of your own finances and plan to support yourself in your old age. You'd assert yourself more. You'd look to as many people as possible to meet your needs for intimacy, caring, and recognition. You'd have a multiplicity of roles and relationships in which you'd invest enough of yourself to insure a good return: worker, volunteer, student, teacher, friend, lover, sibling, daughter, leader, participant. You'd make your own decisions and accept their consequences. Like Peggy.

PEGGY—AN EXAMPLE AND A GIFT

How can you like someone who asks this of her life: that it be "an example and a gift"? Admire, respect, maybe—but *like*? I did, and you would too, if you heard Peggy laughing at herself as the words come out of her mouth. She *is* an example, one of those women who's always turning up on someone's Most Admired list. She is a physician, board certified in four different specialties; with two partners, she operates, staffs, and manages the emergency room of a big-city hospital. When there's a disaster somewhere and you see those newspaper photographs of American medical teams treating the survivors, in Armenia or Nicaragua, Peggy's in the picture. If you hear about a group making a try for the summit of a mountain in Alaska, Peggy's probably in it. She's on the board of a half dozen organizations, professional and civic, and when slick city magazines nominate The Women Whom (You'd Like to Know, Date, Be Stuck in Traffic with, Know the Real Dirt On, Fix Up with Your Best Friend, etc.), Peggy's name will come up. She's short, dark, peppy, and impressively fit—"I was in training to be tall and blond, but it didn't work," she says, "so I work out. Having the healthiest cardiovascular system I can have is a *commitment* to me." She's turned out in a size negligible wool-jersey dress that makes it perfectly clear there are other benefits to disciplined, regular exercise besides a well-muscled heart, and when she giggles, she does it with her whole terrific body.

And then she goes on to make more statements: She says things like, "When possibility is present, so is excitement," and talks about "the conversation you create about your life"—perfectly logical answers to questions I haven't asked yet, but by which I recognize that Peggy is coming from somewhere, as they say on the West Coast, or has an attitude, as they say in the East. I don't know what they say in the rest of the country, but Peggy is delighted to confirm it, and tell you how EST changed her life. Well, everybody's got to have something, I tell myself; after all, remember how John sounded right after he went to A.A.—the jargon? And how Clio was when she was in psychoanalysis? And Aunt Maude when she got "born again"? And Judy, after she took assertiveness training? And me, too, of course, the last time I found a new paradigm, another way of looking at the world and experiencing myself in it. (For me it was Weight Watchers, but you get the idea.)

It doesn't take long to translate from Peggy's particular jargon into realspeak—Peggy makes fun of it herself. And her statements are clear and direct, her enthusiasm contagious and engaging. It's not her particular context that appeals to me, but the very real enrichment and excitement she gets from it, which makes me think, *I could feel that way, too—didn't I used to? About something?*

Peggy remembers her childhood as isolating, lonely, not very satisfying. Her parents loved her, but were distant. They put value on accomplishment, but not engagement. She spent a lot of her youth achieving, not much of it relating. "I conceptualized myself as a loner; that was my image of myself in the world. I didn't like it—inside I was pretty chaotic emotionally—but I lived it. I wasn't socialized to see the value of other people; friendship, as such, was a waste of time. That's how it was in my family, although of course my culture was telling me something very different, the way it tells all girls that relationships matter more than accomplishment." When people ask her why she's been single for all her thirty-eight years, she used to quote Gloria Steinem; "I don't mate in captivity." It made women nod in agreement and men come on to her, she says ruefully now. But what she really meant was that she didn't see the utilitarian value of a husband. Not only didn't she need one, she didn't want one. "I felt fear about it, too—I still do. I'm afraid it would be boring, stultifying, limiting, a brake on my freedom to accomplish all that I want to do." And then her face softens, and she smiles and says, "But that's only my story about marriage. I can find plenty of evidence to support that story if I choose to. Or I can change my story." She's working on it; she says that marriage—and a child—are now in the Project stage, which she hopes to move soon to Commitment, which will provide the Power and Optimism to make it happen.

(*Sure*, I tell myself, and then I remember an evening I spent a few years ago when I was writing *Women on Top* with three women, in their mid-thirties then, women of accomplishment who sounded a lot like Peggy, even though they didn't Capitalize their Commitments. They all said they wanted to get married and have a baby in the next five years. "I worked fifteen years for these five, and I'm going to make them count," said Claudia. To whom I sent a baby gift last year, as I sent one each to Marilyn and to Pepper. I wrote then that "Women on Top use the same focused consciousness, the same abilities to strategize and actualize that got them this far professionally, in pursuing their more personal goals.")

"I think I haven't married, up to this point, simply to prove that I didn't have to," Peggy says. "That's what I was up against—that conditioning that says a woman *must*. There's a part of me that really rebelled against that." Maybe because she was lonely as a kid, she needs people more now—"college, medical school, they were wonderful, because of the collegiality. The friendships. The struggling together. I needed to experience a lot of people in my life. And I have. I've had good relationships with men, but they were always self-limiting—they lasted a year and then *phfft!* they were over. It was never a big deal, even when I was madly in love. That was part of my story—I didn't need anyone. I know better now. Solitude is still important to me—I'd still rather climb a mountain by myself than with company. Yet I don't consider myself a loner at all. Even when there's no one else, I'm connected in a deeper sense to others, and without others, there's nothing, not in a personal sense and not in a global, interrelated sense, that is absolutely necessary to survival. My commitment is to connection. I would like it to be to a husband, a child, but I'll still be connected if it's not to that."

All of Peggy's commitments have this in common: She can do them. There's no *until* stopping her. Her context is one of possibility and transformation; both happen, she says, when she can detach from a specific fantasy of how her life is going to look and let her commitment be her guide. A commitment requires knowing what the conditions are for satisfaction, and by when—that is, what it will take to make it happen, and how long, a kind of mental bottom line. "Nothing happens until then—until then, it's just a fantasy," Peggy says. "A certain amount of daydreaming is necessary—that's where vision comes from, then goals, ways to get from here to there. Some people call it visualization. Between fantasy and commitment, a lot has to happen. You really have to be able to see it, know where the energy will come from to make it happen, who will help you, what you need to do or to have to get started, what the probabilities for breakdown are." And then she drops another EST-ism into the conversation: "A breakdown is nothing but an opportunity for a breakthrough." But at least she laughs.

Peggy has thought a great deal about wanting and waiting and the difference between them. If she really wants something, she only waits until the how and when are clear. Meanwhile, she focuses on what she can get through her own efforts, keeping her eyes open for what can happen when she lets go of the fantasy of how her life should look, inhabiting it fully and happily, rarely considering the possibility of failure of either will or accomplishment. "I'd rather think about the problems of having it all—like, where would I *put* it?" she laughs.

This is what I learned from Peggy: *There's a difference between fantasy and commitment. Though both may be created and nurtured in solitude, commitment demands connection, with the self, and with the world beyond it, using action and will to accomplish what you want. Every change begins with a fantasy—an image of what might happen If. When we are locked into a fantasy of the Other, change is dependent on him. When we have a fantasy of our possible selves, change depends only on us. A fantasy can suggest a commitment and energize a goal, but cannot, by itself, really make it happen.*

❄ 4 ❄

Getting Down to Business

A decade ago I crisscrossed the country, talking to working women about success—not how they achieved it, but what it *felt* like and how it changed their lives. My recent experience with success was changing my own life, not always in wholly positive ways; when Gail Sheehy told me, "Success isn't as bad as a case of chronic bursitis, but it isn't the golden dream, either," I knew what she meant. Success seemed to have altered other people's perception of me; moreover, it was changing the way I felt about myself, too. I had ideas, feelings, and ambitions that didn't square with who I was, or thought I was—I didn't know the person I seemed to be becoming. So I set out to find new role models, new heroines. Looking back at that time now, I think that, deep in my heart, I'd expected, even wanted, to discover that career achievement for women exacted too high a price. That successful women paid for their power suits, their Gucci pumps, with their personal lives. That the prestige, the big bucks, the title on the door or the byline on the book cost more than I would ever want to pay in terms of friends, family, freedom, and yes, femininity.

A few months before, I had gone from being a free-lance copywriter and part-time journalist to a nationally published author. It was what Gail Sheehy called a radioactive time—it happened to her when *Passages*, the ground-breaking book that made

"mid-life crisis" a household phrase, was published. My own publishing debut was much more modest, but there were enough
parallels between her experience and mine to make my interviews
with her more personally fascinating than any of the others I
undertook for *Women On Top*. I had more in common with Gail
than I did with the company presidents and other executives,
entrepreneurs, lawyers, politicians, educators, and producers who
shared their lives and feelings with me. She and I were contem-
poraries, journalists with similar backgrounds, situations, and a
common interest in how people respond to social change. Success
had seemed to happen to her, as it had to me, by default. Like me,
she'd mostly been engaged in simply trying to survive and earn a
living, while raising a child alone. She never really thought about
her work as a career, she told me, until she had one. Neither had
I. Writing was what I did to pay the bills while I waited for
someone to rescue me.

Before I married, I'd had a job that thrilled, excited, and totally
engaged me. In Washington during the Kennedy era, I worked as
a speechwriter and press secretary for a politician I admired, and
felt part of a movement and one with people I believed might
truly change the world. And then I followed my new husband
west, leaving behind my sense of purpose, self-esteem, compe-
tence, and connectivity. Supported by a husband, I settled into
domesticity and waited to get pregnant. When it didn't happen
on schedule, and I'd bored myself silly, I went looking for a job.
I drifted into copywriting—it was painless, pleasant, and didn't
interfere with what I considered my "real" life. It brought me
money—not "real" money, which was what men earned, but pin
money, which I spent with great pleasure and such abandon that
I often had to wheedle enough from my husband to pay my credit
card bills. When I felt like taking a day off, I did—my efforts
didn't matter that much, and anyone could do what I did. If
enough monkeys sat at enough typewriters long enough, I told
my friends, they'd eventually write good budget-floor white-sale
copy, too. I thought I'd quit when I had a baby, and then I would

do *that* for a while, until some hazy time in the future, when I would turn the nursery into a study—in tones of soft gray, I thought, with Wedgewood-blue accents—and in those hours when I wasn't giving elegant dinners for my husband's business associates, or driving my kids to band practice, I would retreat to it and write the Great American Novel.

I did quit when I got pregnant; when the marriage collapsed five years later, leaving me with two children to support, I was way too desperate to think about a career. What I needed was a living, which was copywriting, but it wasn't fun anymore—it was simply a paycheck. I wrote ads for products I didn't believe in, worked in an industry I didn't respect, with people I didn't like, and somehow I must have thought I deserved it—after all, I'd failed at the only real career this Sleeping Beauty had ever expected to have.

I considered the job only temporary; soon I would marry again, soon someone would save me. Two years later no one had shown up, not to stay, anyway. I had begun not only to resent but to actively hate what I did for eight long hours every day. What finally drove me to quit was not failure, but success—of a sort. I had created an entire ad campaign for a recreational property development I'd never even seen firsthand; I had a few sketchy architectural drawings and the client's specs, but I didn't care enough to visit the site, which was less than an hour's drive away. It seemed like enough effort, and it must have been—the campaign won numerous awards and the client was delighted. With the bonus I earned, I went skiing. On the way to the slopes, I passed the development I'd praised so lavishly in my copy. It was a blot on the landscape—a clear-cut mountainside stripped of trees, eroded and barren, covered with cheap, tacky little houses on which the paint was already beginning to peel. I felt embarrassed, ashamed, and defensive; I had no choice, I told myself, but another voice inside me, the voice of my conscience, answered, *Sure you did. You just made the wrong one.*

I quit the agency the next month and began free-lancing. I still didn't like what I was doing, but at least I had some freedom to choose my clients, and I could call my time my own. Then I began to write part-time for a new city newspaper. It didn't pay much more than self-respect, but that was sufficient. The by-lines mattered more than money; the pleasure of doing something I liked, was good at, among people I respected, was what counted. Advertising paid the bills, journalism fed my soul. And then I wrote a cover story about something that was a problem in my life and the lives of many people I knew—about how to be a single parent and still be a sexual human being. Out of that came a book contract, a television movie, and then national assignments and lectures; suddenly, I had what was beginning to look like a career.

It was very exhilarating, but frightening, too, especially when I let the copywriting go. What if I couldn't do it? What if I couldn't write a second book? What if the lectures stopped, the assignments tapered off, the money ran out, and no one appeared to rescue me from my own recklessness? And what if the worst didn't happen, but the best did? What if I got to be a big success? What would my life be like then? So my second book, *Women on Top*, like my first, *Sex and the Single Parent*, was an attempt to clarify my experience by writing about it; to learn what I needed to know from women who were dealing with change—professional rather than personal this time, although it was the human, relational side of career achievement that interested me more than the effective, instrumental side—the feeling, not the doing.

By the time I interviewed Gail Sheehy, I had had to dispense with my preconceived notions about women and success. The women I'd met had made choices, not sacrifices. They'd paid some prices, but none they couldn't afford, as one CEO put it. And achievement not only had its rewards, it *was* the reward. It put women in control of their own lives—and the more in control they were, the happier they seemed to be. As Baruch, Barnett, and Rivers reported in *Lifeprints*,[1] my interviewees had a stable, intact sense of self connected to their work rather than to their relationships—even the happily married ones. And those who weren't married could tolerate some dissatisfaction in their love lives without getting anxious or depressed. Their self-esteem, the meaning they found in their work, and their excellence at it, carried them through emotionally rocky periods. Like all women who work at jobs that offer challenge, stimulation, a variety of tasks, a chance to learn, a good fit with their skills and talents, and occasions to make decisions, the careers of these women on top gave them an opportunity "to change and grow as adults—to be able to transform or transcend the recurrent moments of stagnation, confinement, and aborted promise . . . a sense of purpose, the feeling of being in control of their lives, in a position to make choices that will work out over a lifetime in such a way that identity is extended, elaborated, and renewed."[2]

Of all the things Gail Sheehy told me, the words I remember most clearly, that seemed to have the most relevance to my own life, described a time—moments, hours, days—when she was so absorbed in doing work she loved that nothing else seemed to matter. The Greeks call it *kairos*, a oneness with self in which concentration is so total that time itself seems not to exist because you are participating in it. "The fact that there is another, compelling world for a woman—in my case, the world of ideas—an engrossing, surging, passionate, almost sexual feeling that comes when you are with your project—is difficult for most people, even those you love, to accept," Sheehy said. "Men, and even children, are an intrusion, and there's no use pretending they aren't." For her that passion generated a need to live up to a capacity she never knew she had—a need that, once aroused, could no longer be ignored.

I had experienced that absorption, felt the stirring of that need, too, and it scared me. What if the Prince arrived, and I was so engrossed in my work that I didn't hear the doorbell ring? What if I made such a commitment to career that my personal life went to hell? What if I began to value work, not for the money or even the success, *but for its own sake*? What man would want me then?

SLEEPING ON THE JOB

What are women who've made a less than wholehearted career commitment waiting for? What holds them back? What keeps them marking time at jobs that don't fulfill, challenge, or enrich them?

It could be Small Mind, making assumptions or creating expectations based on the past and the future rather than the present. Because Small Mind doesn't make distinctions about situations, only feelings, professional procrastination may be tied to experience that seems unconnected to a woman's work history— to childhood, for instance, when even though you knew the answers you had to wait until the teacher called on you; when you climbed out onto the farthest limb of the tree in the backyard, and fell out and broke your arm; when you did all the work building the fort in the woods, and your brothers wouldn't let you use it; when you learned it wasn't OK to ask for credit for your efforts, it wasn't smart to stick your neck out, it wasn't popular to be intelligent; when you learned it was better to be safe than sorry, wiser to be patient than hasty, more acceptable to be accommodating instead of confrontive.

Bellamy, a personnel manager, is staying in a job that gives her ulcers because she thinks it will get better as soon as her boss leaves. After all, she was happy enough under her previous boss, and even though the new one seems settled in for the duration, she says, "If you wait long enough, anything can happen."

Sandy, whose company is the target of takeover rumors, is pinning her hopes on a change in the corporate culture that might make her work environment more humane, more in tune with her personal values. There's an equally good chance that the new owners will be worse—raiders don't often have agendas for social change in mind—"But you never can tell," says Sandy. Darlene is waiting until someone tells her what to do—the last time she took the initiative in a job, she made a mistake that cost her a promotion. And Ellen, who pops a tranquilizer every morning before she leaves for the office, says that one of these days the stress will really get to her; "I'll blow my top, and then they'll fire me," she says.

Some Sleeping Beauties wait passively throughout their working lives because of Big Mind's inhibitions against acting in ways that conflict with gender conditioning. They wait for promotions—it's not OK to ask. They wait to be chosen—it's pushy and manlike to assert themselves. They wait for someone to tell them what to do—someone else always knows better. They wait for approval—for a man to say they're doing a good job. They wait for the right time—when everyone else's needs have been met. They wait to take action until everyone agrees. They wait for corroboration of their authority. For protection. For titles, power, and pay.

Some Sleeping Beauties can't get down to business because they feel a conflict between their personal values or ethics and the product, service, mission, or environment that the job or profession promotes. When there is a clash between context and career, they wait—for the system to change, for a deteriorating situation to improve, for others to share their moral indignation.

Most of all, Sleeping Beauties who are stuck in their jobs wait for five o'clock to roll around. Real life isn't in the office—real life is later, when human relationship needs take precedence over profit or efficiency, when being good, respectful, or helpless will get them what they deserve, when they don't have to compete to win, when they can react rather than act, when people are open and honest rather than manipulative and calculating, when they never have to stick their necks out or risk being wrong.

Janice LaRouche, author of *Strategies for Women at Work*, believes that problems at work come from the same passive attitudes that plague Sleeping Beauties in other areas of their lives. They are too chaste, too moral, too naive, she says; they don't want to learn the ways of the working world because they think and hope they won't be in it much longer. They put themselves down and push others up—the less they believe in their ability to do things for themselves, the more they believe in the power of others to do things for them. They wait for things to happen to them because they're still ambivalent about working in the first place. They wait for answers, apologies, information, and attention. And, most of all, they wait for everything to be better. "To risk being wrong is to risk being without value—perfection is the only ticket to acceptance," writes LaRouche. "It's as if we believe that whatever we have to give is not enough—our value is not sufficient to offset our errors."[3]

So what are you waiting for? Until someone else defines the job's limits, boundaries, or responsibilities? Until you can do it perfectly? Until someone else brings up an idea you can use? Until someone gives you permission to act? Until you get answers to your questions, recognition of your feelings, or your boss's attention?

How much longer are you going to wait?

THE RIGHT PLACE AT THE RIGHT TIME

Many Sleeping Beauties stake out a place in the business world and wait for lightning to strike. The last time that happened was nearly twenty years ago, when affirmative action propelled many women into visible, if not always viable, jobs and responsibilities that had previously been closed to them. Many successful women of that generation credited good timing with getting them where they were—only a few were willing to admit that they'd worked, pushed, or persuaded their way into the boardroom with skill, sacrifice, and perseverance. "Somehow you had to make it look easy," said Angela, vice president of a Fortune 500 company. "You couldn't admit that, in fact, it wasn't easy at all. You know that old saying that horses sweat, men perspire, and women glow? Well, you had to glow."

Sleeping Beauties need to glow because it isn't feminine to sweat over work. Because it isn't worth getting lathered over—it's just a job. When their professional lives are difficult, stressful, or unrewarding, they look to the other areas of their lives to make up for it. It's what the authors of *Lifeprints* call the wrong place syndrome; they're looking in the wrong place—their relationships—to get the strokes, satisfaction, and rewards that are more readily available in their other arenas. "Women too often misunderstand the sources of their own well-being," say these experts. "When they are depressed they turn to their relationships, but this is not always an area in which they feel in control of their lives or get their self-esteem. When the real problem is in the area of Mastery, a changed relationship won't really change [a woman's] life . . . she would go from being a woman without a man who felt bad about herself to being a woman with a man who felt bad about herself, or she would change from an unhappy non-mother to an unhappy mother."[4]

By exaggerating love and undervaluing work, Sleeping Beauty sets herself up for unhappiness. She narrows the base for her sense of well-being, and ties it to the approval of others—most often, a man. But any place can be the right place, and any time can be the right time, for women who are willing to believe something that goes against everything we've been taught: "that work is real life, that a professional identity is a stable, not a transitional, one."[5]

When you make *this* time the right time and *this* or some other place the right place, your career provides you with a stronger sense of identity than any other aspect of your life. When you are fully present in a job you have consciously chosen to do, when you know that your efforts make a difference and your actions matter, your work may change, but your self remains whole, and exists in what you do. In work, as in love, as psychiatrist Thomas Szasz says, "the issue is not whether or not we have found ourselves, but whether or not we have *created* ourselves." When Sleeping Beauty taps into her open mind, she discovers the potential of her work to generate vitality and express the capable, congruent, connected woman who slumbers within her.

THE WAY TO GET FROM HERE TO THERE

A lecturer on entrepreneurship at the graduate school of management at UCLA tells this story from "Alice in Wonderland" to his classes on small-business development:

Alice:	Would you tell me, please, which way I ought to go from here?
Cheshire Cat:	That depends a good deal on where you want to get to.
Alice:	I don't much care where . . .
Cheshire Cat:	Then it doesn't matter which way you go.
Alice	. . . so long as I get *somewhere*.
Cheshire Cat:	Oh, you're sure to do that if only you walk long enough.[6]

If you've been sleeping on the job for longer than you should, it may be time to consider whether you are, in fact, in the right place; to ask yourself what you're waiting for and realistically assess your chances for getting it; to decide if you need to change the job, or the way you act in it; to see if you should change the direction, focus, or content of your career; to wonder if your intelligence, training, skills, talents, energy, and aspirations could be put to better use somewhere else.

Are you oriented to people, but working with data? Happier with projects, but saddled with tasks? In a setting that hinders or promotes your power, creativity, and values? Are you in the public sector when the private side appeals to you? Wearing a managerial suit beneath which beats the soul of an entrepreneur? Working alone when you're happiest surrounded by others? In a staff job when you crave the bottom line?

Looking at what you have and want from your job is another way to experience yourself, check the fit between context and career, the congruence between who you are and what you do. Often women have chosen careers either because of what was available when they went looking, or because they never expected to do it for a lifetime, or because someone told them it was a good field for a woman, or because it was a "hot" field when they finished college. Times, goals, and values have changed, but perhaps those jobs have not. If that's true of yours, maybe you really aren't in the right place, at the right time, in the right livelihood. Think about that for a while. Then sit down and write a job description—not for you, but for your successor—in the job you're doing right now. List all the qualities and abilities you, with your inside knowledge, know are demanded by this job. And then see if they still apply, or ever really applied, to you.

Millie, who works for IBM in a middle-management position, went one step further with this exercise. After she did the first, she wrote another—one that set out the kind of job she wanted to have. She was surprised at the disparity between them. "It was like trying to squeeze a size-eight foot into a size-six shoe," she said. "What my position really requires is a precise, logical, left-brained person who likes tasks that can be completed in a given time frame, working within a defined set of parameters, functioning well in a team setting, with plenty of direction and feedback. Who I am is an extrovert, a generalist rather than a specialist, who likes inspiring people, but not really managing them. I like big ideas rather than small tasks. I chafe in situations where I've got to work inside, in an organizational structure where I'm defined by my job title."

Millie does well at her job, despite the fact that she doesn't really like it. "I stifle my instincts," she says. "To get along, you have to go along. I keep thinking that if I do this job perfectly, someone will see that I'm capable of more. I joined IBM for security, and I have that. But that's all I have. If I were in personnel, I'd never have hired me for this position. I'd have seen the rebel underneath this dress-for-success suit, and sent her on her way."

Sylvia, who got an M.B.A. ten years ago when she saw what M.B.A.s were earning right out of graduate school, knows she's in the wrong place. "I hate this emphasis on profit, profit, profit," she says. "I can't stand being responsible for other people's money—not the firm's, but all the customers'. The hours I work are horrendous. I don't create anything of value. I'm not good at backslapping. I don't mind the number crunching—actually, I enjoy that most of all—but the competitiveness really gets to me. People stab each other in the back here all the time. As soon as I've got enough saved up, I'm quitting. I'd like to work in the nonprofit sector, and as soon as I can afford to, I will." It sounds like a good plan. Except that Sylvia spends right up to her salary, buying herself things to compensate for everything else she's missing in her career, and donating most of her commissions to charity to assuage the guilt she feels at earning more money than her father did in ten years or her boyfriend does in two.

Sylvia is a professional, and she takes pride in that. To her, being a professional means doing a job well, even if she doesn't like it. Her attitude illustrates the double bind of professionalism that traps many working women, who often feel that female-identified values have no place in the business world, and must be relegated to their personal lives. "It seems to be easier for men—or women who are passing as men. They don't seem to be as bothered as I am by the incongruity between their ethics and their work environment, or by how they feel and how they act. I wonder if you can be like them—successful—without *being* like them?" To Sylvia, professional means masculine at worst, neutral at best; in fact, it means blending the attitudes and actions of both sexes, not passing as one or being limited by the other.

There is an enormous discrepancy between what Sylvia thinks her career ought to offer (besides money) and what it actually does provide; between what her skills and interests ought to be and what they truly are. "I don't know why I'm here," she says. "If there is a purpose besides the bottom line, I've lost sight of it."

If there isn't a purpose as well as a payoff for your efforts on the job, you are probably shortchanging yourself. It's your right to define what's important—your right and your power. When you give it away to someone else—your employer, your friends, your family, or your culture—you're being a Sleeping Beauty. What's needed here is career management, and although you may turn to others for help, ultimately you are the one in charge. The kind of personal assessment that's necessary to make a better fit between who you are and what you do has benefits related to other things besides career; it may be an alternative to therapy, an addition to awareness, a key to integrating personal as well as professional satisfactions. Which brings up another point. Many women, in fact, most of us, automatically distinguish love and work in just that fashion—not personal *and* professional, but personal *or* professional. We draw a solid dividing line between those two life environments. In fact, particularly for the single woman, this kind of thinking tends toward a self-defeating dualism that separates one from the other so sharply that it promotes incongruence; it says we can only find challenge in work and pleasure in love. But this isn't true of anyone who loves her career, who lives to work rather than works to live. She finds challenges, excitement, and esteem, emotional as well as intellectual and financial rewards, friends, partners, and sometimes lovers through her career. And when her life on the job is as "real" as her life after hours, she finds caring, creativity, congruence, and connection there, too.

You cannot fully develop your capacities for meaningful work if you function only in your emotions. But your feelings about your job, if you let yourself explore them, can lead you to a more fulfilling career, one that offers you more roles and more possibilities, or a new way of functioning in the work you do now. Opening the doors to awareness in order to discover the truths that can guide you to a greater vocational integration is a beginning. Consider how Small Mind, Big Mind, and, for those fortunate few who see the potential for work as devotion, Great Mind, influence the way you perceive your career. Create a symbol or a metaphor that describes the way you feel about it, and the way you'd like to; when Millie said she thought of her job as a pair of shoes that pinched her feet, she knew it was time to take them off.

Look for heroines who are happy, fulfilled, and empowered by their jobs, women who feel connected to their work in a deep and meaningful way. Learn what the experts know; there are a number of excellent books and articles available on choosing a career, managing a job, and working with passion and pleasure. Be aware that some of the most popular books in this area promote the personal/professional dualism, and others seem to suggest that a working woman has only two choices: being "like them," or being one's self. A few suggest that work is or should be peripheral rather than central to a woman's life, or assume that all women are afraid of success or have a compromised commitment to their careers. Of course there are some issues that are especially relevant to women, but often books that are gender-neutral on professional development suggest more strategies and possibilities than those addressed strictly to women.

In addition to books, there are career workshops, seminars, and development programs that can help you focus on remaking your work so that it provides the life and meaning you desire. Approach vocational aptitude tests with caution; too often they simply reinforce your old, outdated notions of self rather than reflect the person you have become after a few years on the job. Test what you read, learn, and hear against your own experience as well as your intuition; the process of defining and refining your career context, goals, and accomplishments may result in no change except an internal one, but that can be the most important change of all.

All this information can guide you to a new investment in a richer, happier, more integrated approach to your career, especially whatever helps clarify your attitudes and values; but that doesn't mean abandoning your own choice, your own authority, to experts. Understand that the process of coming to terms with career may take years. It is another way of knowing yourself, and that doesn't happen overnight. But don't wait forever to be sure of the next step—drag it out too long and it becomes an excuse for not doing anything at all. Be guided by your own instincts, and consider the teachings of Buddha on Right Livelihood: Work that is consciously chosen, and done with full awareness and care, will always lead to enlightenment.

DEBORAH—A LIFE IN TRANSITION

When I read *The New York Times* article about workshops for lawyers in transition, I remembered the attorney who had come to me two years before for advice on writing a book on just that topic. I even remembered the title, which I'd thought particularly apt: *Running from the Law.* According to the newspaper, Deborah had finally done just that, and the book was due to be published in the next month. So we made a date to meet and talk about the process that changed not only Deborah's job, but also her life.

When I first met Deborah, she was a few months past the real breaking point—giving up her legal practice. There had been earlier attempts to remake her career; she was trying to satisfy her growing feeling that she was somehow "not doing it right." Just short of partnership with a prestigious firm six years before, she'd gone into practice with a man who was her best friend, the most important person in her life—"not my lover, not my husband, but in many ways, it was like a marriage, a bad one . . . he screwed up, I bailed him out. He brought in the clients, I did the work. It was a dysfunctional partnership, and I was a codependent, although I didn't know it then. Ending the partnership, though, never addressed the real issue for me, which wasn't about *how* I practiced law, but *why*," Deborah said. "When I quit practicing, I asked myself, *Why am I here? What's my reason for living?* I said, *If I can find one good one, I'll stick with it.* The whole reason for going into it in the first place was to please other people, especially my parents. I was never really motivated by money, but at the end, that was all it was good for. The rest of it was meaningless—I felt spiritually bankrupt."

She had no idea what spiritually full meant, she added: "I knew it didn't mean religion, didn't mean being reborn or joining a church, but I knew it had something to do with meaning in life, and if I could just figure out my purpose, why I was on earth, I'd be OK."

Like a squirrel storing nuts against a winter she knew would eventually arrive, Deborah had been saving money for several years. "I decided to invest in change, and, more important, how much I could afford to invest," she said. She didn't touch her retirement account, but she cut her spending drastically the last year of her practice and watched her bank account fatten. The market was up, she sold her house at a hefty profit, and her money "just changed location—in the three years since I did this, my net worth is exactly the same as it was then. Once I decided to make a change, it was important for me to put a price tag on it."

In that last year as an attorney, she went to career workshops, sought advice from others, and read a number of books that clarified what it was she was seeking. She also looked for role models, and found them in unusual places. "For instance, I really admired Shirley MacLaine—she's undisturbed by convention, she's a strong personality, and even though some of her concepts are way too airy-fairy for me, I admired her for expressing herself. And I met a former practicing attorney who'd made the kind of career change I was looking for, who believed you could have it all, and convinced me I could, too."

The quality of Deborah's relationships provided a further clue to the change she wanted to make. "A man I really trusted described the way I interacted with men in terms that made perfect sense to a lawyer—controlling, manipulative, strategic, adversarial—but none at all in any other part of my life. I felt that I couldn't be the person I knew underneath I was—in a word, *nice*—and still be a practicing attorney. I couldn't act one way at work and another in the rest of my life. It made me crazy," said Deborah.

She "got into Overeaters Anonymous, and all that Twelve-Step stuff made sense." She took Context training, which is similar to EST, in that it uses a variety of techniques that help people focus on what they really want out of life, and suggests attitudes and behaviors that hinder or block satisfaction. "It made me look at my beliefs and values like a grid or screen and realize that the slightest shift in that screen causes you to perceive things differently. I learned that I had the absolute power to create what I wanted in life, and that my purpose was to create the life I wanted to lead." Deborah had mistrusted the idea of "so-called transformation training," as she put it. "But this program seemed to have integrity. For one thing, they give your money back if you're not satisfied. So I gave it a try. What I came up with was that what I really wanted were these things: freedom to pursue my other interests; a home environment that had a family feeling to it; a healthier way to live. So over the next year I created it."

She sold one house and bought another, larger one, which she filled with housemates who gave her that "family feeling." She finished up her professional obligations, vowing to spend only four billable hours a day doing them. She traveled. She gardened. She puttered in her house. And she stayed active in the Bar Association—"I wanted to work with lawyers, I just didn't want to practice with them," she said. Ultimately, she had what she describes, blushingly, as a vision. "When I kept asking myself, *Why are you on earth?* I finally got an answer. A peacemaker. That was what my deepest self told me—I was here to make peace. I was able to visualize a world where people expressed love, worked together, supported one another, did beautiful and wonderful things. The vision was so powerful it made me cry, but it allowed me to be what I was, express my unconventional spirit, try things no one else thought made any sense, be out on the edge. It touched a deep well in me; it was like looking down into water so clear you can see what's at the bottom. I couldn't understand why people didn't live that way."

Wanting to be with people who supported one another led Deborah to the formation of "Lawyers in Transition," where legal professionals help each other through the process of change, not always out of the profession, but often with a different perspective about the law—"a slight shift in the screen that makes all the difference." In one of the first workshops she led, another attorney came up with the metaphor that fit her own experience to a tee: "Practicing law is a nightmare; I'd like to wake up, but I need the sleep."

Deborah isn't grandiosely idealistic. "I knew I wanted my life to have impact, to make a difference in others' lives. If I measure that by whether there's peace in the world by the time I die, I'll probably feel a tremendous sense of failure then. But if I'm going to look at whether I've lived my life in a way that's consistent with what I believe, then I'll feel like a great success, because I will have created peace within myself and harmony among some of my peers."

In other areas of Deborah's life, change has worked from the inside out, too. After an adult lifetime of codependent relationships with men, she gave up "the romantic package men came in—the crazy, passionate, painful one. I gave up the fantasy of the perfect romance and found a real relationship instead." And then she added, "In life, in love, and in work, I've stopped waiting. I've given up the struggle."

Deborah is thirty-eight, and when I asked her what else she'd waited for, she grinned, and her dark eyes sparkled. "I waited to be thin all my life," she said. "I always thought I'd find a perfect man when I was thin. I'd have a career on television when I was thin. I'd buy fabulous clothes when I was thin. I'd have a wonderful sex life when I was thin. I waited till I had enough of awfulness—enough pain, enough unhappiness. That point was always when I absolutely couldn't take it anymore, till I was too miserable not to do something that needed doing. That was true of my career, true of my relationships, true of my destructive patterns. I guess I waited for permission, although from whom I don't know—my family, my culture, my profession. I waited for permission to get off the partner track, to give up practicing law, to be loving and sexual, to be spontaneous, to make my work and my life one seamless, beautiful garment."

That dualism that divides work and life for many women was expressed by Deborah's closet back in the days when she appeared regularly in court. "It was like a schizophrenic's wardrobe . . . on one side here were all these severe gray and navy suits and sensible shoes, and on the other were blouses of soft fabrics, skirts in glowing colors—loose, sensual things. And every morning I had to decide not only what I was going to wear, but who I was going to be."

These days Deborah knows who she is: a peacemaker, provocateur, and agent of change and growth, with one set of clothes for her whole life. Ellen Goodman once wrote, "There are times when we all end up completing a day, a week, or a month as though it were a task to be crosed off with a sigh." Deborah isn't crossing them off any longer.

What I learned from her is what Thoreau said, of which she reminded me: *"The true cost of a thing is the amount of what I call 'life' which is required to be exchanged for it—immediately, or in the long run."*

SHORTCHANGING YOUR CAREER FOR SOMEONE WHO MIGHT NEVER APPEAR

In the years since writing *Women on Top*, I have interviewed hundreds of other women about their careers. All of them mentioned a moment of confrontation with their ambition, with their feelings about how important they would let work be to them; a time when, as Carrie, a filmmaker, put it, "the genie escaped from the bottle and said, 'I'll give you your wish, but you'll have to give something up. You decide.' "

Carrie, at thirty-four, was at a crossroads in her career. She had an opportunity to make an important documentary film that meant a two-year commitment to a project that would take her ten thousand miles away from home, jeopardize her financial security, and probably end the relationship she'd been in for a year and a half. "There were no guarantees. I could fail dramatically, I could go broke, I could lose my lover," she said. "I could wait until I felt confident I could do the job—the chance came up before I really felt professionally ready to meet it. I could wait until all the details were in place, until all the risks involved were minimized. I could wait for the right time—until I'd satisfied everyone else's needs. And in the end, that's what I decided to do."

Someone else took the risk, "and flopped in a big way," said Carrie, chewing the end of her russet-colored ponytail, her brows knitting together across her broad, unlined forehead. We sat over cappuccino in a Greenwich Village café, and it was clear that thinking about that time still bothered her. In her place another woman might have felt vindicated by the project's eventual failure—it was abandoned half finished. Another woman might have taken pride in her prescience—it had been right to turn down the project, it was ill-fated from the beginning. Another woman might have been glad that someone else, not she, had failed.

But Carrie thinks she failed, too. "I think a lot about whether I could have turned it around, and I still don't know," she told me. "That isn't what matters, though. What does is that here it is, four years later, and I'm still paying for not trying. There's another, similar documentary in the works and with my background, I thought I'd get a shot at it. I waited and waited and finally I called the producer and said, what about me? He said, 'I don't see you as being motivated enough to stay in this business for the long haul; it's not really central to your life.' The job went to a friend of mine, Chris, the same woman who took on the film that flopped last time, but she's getting another chance."

I asked Carrie how she felt about that. She'd talked a great deal about how competitive her industry is, and yet she spoke graciously and fondly about the rival who'd gotten the green light on a film she herself had very much wanted to make.

"I'd like to tell you that she's a professional success but a personal failure," Carrie said, wrinkling her freckled nose. "That's the stereotype, right? Tell you she's got money and power and credits but nothing else, that she sacrificed everything important just to get ahead? Well, I'd like to believe it. That way I could make my own failure to have at least tried more acceptable to me. The fact is, she's a terrific person. She's been in a real struggle the last few years, and she still gets malaria attacks, a lovely souvenir of her months in the jungle trying to make that other film. She's used up all her savings and she's broke, but she's really happy. She met a guy on that shoot, and they're still together."

Carrie and Chris knew each other slightly when they were both being considered for that first film, and they've gotten to be closer since then. "Our careers were pretty much on the same track up until that point," Carrie said, "except I think she was always more committed to her career than I was. She took a longer view. When she didn't get a job, she'd say, 'Well, I'm going to be in this business all my life, one I miss now is one I'll get later.' When Chris went after that film—after I'd turned it down, by the way—there was no guy in her life. She didn't have a steady job in the industry, which I did. I'd taken a risk once before, early on, and when that fell through, it took me a year to find work. I remembered how depressing that year was—I didn't think I could go through it again. So it was easy to rationalize turning down the project and staying where I was—a bird in hand, you know. Besides, there was Tim, and I wanted to get married. I figured if I stuck around, sooner or later he'd make a commitment. And if he didn't, I'd be somewhere I could find someone else, not off in a jungle buried in work. Actually, I was scared I couldn't do it. I wasn't ready. I didn't think I could hack it, and everyone was telling me to wait for a better opportunity. Tim was completely against it. When I told Chris that, she just shrugged. She said, 'You're shortchanging your life for someone who might never come through.' She was right. My relationship broke up, my career dead-ended, and I'm not at a crossroads anymore, I'm at a standstill. I don't feel in control of myself or my life. I don't know if I'll ever get a chance like that again."

Most of us don't confront choices as clear as Carrie's in our professional lives. But Chris's words about shortchanging a career for someone who might never come through, or show up, resonate in the hearts of other women who let opportunities for advancement, excitement, and excellence pass them by; Sleeping Beauties who have been and are still waiting for someone or something to give their lives meaning and ignoring the likeliest place to find it—in their work.

Friendship Is a Category
You Invent Yourself

Remember being sick enough to stay home from school when you were a kid, but not so sick you couldn't enjoy it? On those days, after my father left for the office, I used to crawl into bed with my mother and listen as she made her morning phone calls to her friends. Since that was before liberation, sometimes there was good old catty gossip (during which she always suggested that I go check and see if the mail had arrived yet), but mostly she and her friends shared the less compelling details of their world: what to wear to the bridge luncheon, whether to go to the Cape for vacation, if they should get a real estate license or put their names on the substitute teacher list. "You just saw Aunt Harriet yesterday," I said once, after one of those calls. "How can you spend an hour talking about nothing?"

My mother smiled indulgently. "I hope when you're my age you'll have friends you can talk to all morning about *nothing*."

Now I do, although most of my friends, men and women, don't have the time. Peggy has her sales meeting on Monday morning, and Kate is in trial this week. Sean's on the day shift at the hospital, and Carol's in San Francisco for a conference. Marion has patient hours until seven this evening, Britt has her hands full with the twins, and Allan's got end-of-term conferences all week.

So much for the A list. Still, there are others I can reach out and touch if I'm really not ready to settle down to work yet. Not my nearest and dearest, but not a disembodied voice at the end of an 800 number, either. There's my "exchange"—the network of not very intimate but nonetheless satisfying friends and acquaintances with whom I do or trade favors, activities, connections, and information. Like Jerry, my tennis partner. After we play, we usually have a drink and talk about the game, mutual friends, our jobs, but it's all on a very casual level, which is OK with me. I once thought Jerry had the potential for more, but that turned out not to be the case. The slight buzz I felt in his presence when we first met has disappeared—without ever talking about it, the sexual chemistry evaporated. He's engaged now, and while I'm happy for him, it leaves me wondering where I'll find somebody else who'll put up with my erratic game and won't sue me the next time my racket flies out of my hand and whomps him on the side of the head.

I could call Don. He's a journalist I used to know slightly, and a year ago I sent what turned out to be a good story his way. Since then, he's returned the favor a couple of times. We are what he calls "old inactives"—we met a long time ago, were close for a while, and then drifted apart. When he called last year I hadn't seen him in over a decade, but we've renewed our relationship and discovered that since our life situations and careers have changed, we have more in common than we once did. And also that we're both single. I know it's not going to be a great romance, but it might be a good, durable friendship.

I should get in touch with Kathleen, who's a realtor. Some friends I met on vacation are planning to move here and are looking for a house; Kathleen sold mine for me, and she'd do a good job for them. When I was selling my house, I'd just taken up diving. She listened to me rave about it, and got certified herself, following which we took a diving vacation together. We've been pals ever since—close, but not tight, although our friendship is growing as we learn to accept each other's differences. Still, I know her better than I do Jeanette, whom I met at a political meeting a few weeks ago; we seemed to hit it off, and traded "let's have lunch" good-byes. I didn't think then that we'd ever be bosom buddies, but you never can tell, and meanwhile we have at least one shared interest to build on.

Then there's the list of people I *need* to call: my editor, the dentist, the chair of the planning committee, my travel agent. Before I know it, the morning has slipped away in the kind of phone calls I might have dismissed as "nothing" when I was too young to know better. None of these conversations was with a close, intimate friend, but they serve an equally important function: They are connections to the world, connections that matter particularly if one works alone, as I often do. The Sleeping Beauty in me is frequently envious of those who have a more well-defined work matrix than mine; it seems easier for them to meet people, to expand their circle of friends and acquaintances. For them, it seems to just happen; I have to work at it, and sometimes I resent it. When I don't, my world narrows, and I begin to feel lonely. Sometimes I feel like a hamster spinning on a wheel in his cage; if I stopped pedaling, I wonder, would anyone notice? Would anything happen? If I didn't constantly put energy into friendships, would I have any? And when is it some other hamster's turn to pedal?

When I share those feelings with Barbara, an organizational anthropologist who spends a few weeks or months immersed in one corporate culture then moves on to another, she says, "Well, yes, but although I *see* a lot of people, I don't really *meet* all that many. And even those I really *meet* I don't often *know*."

Meeting, seeing, and knowing are three different aspects of connection. And intimate connections, while they are central to feelings of self-esteem, are not the only ones that spell relatedness. Psychotherapist Marvin Thomas uses the metaphor of village to denote the relationship between self and connection. "The heart of the village is the personal village—the autonomous self," he says. "Radiating out from that, in a series of often overlapping circles, is a collection of people, intimate and nonintimate, who make up one's cadre." A cadre is a supportive community that exists not just to answer intrinsic needs for connection, but because, says Thomas, "Life is simply too complex to be lived alone. We have come to depend on professionals to answer needs in every area of our lives, rather than amateurs—our friends." As a practicing therapist for two decades, he has seen a growing trend toward "consulting someone like me—not for reasons of serious emotional problems that really need professional intervention, but for the kind of self-disclosing intimacy, willingness to risk vulnerability, that a caring and attentive friendship could as easily provide."

I first met Marv in an encounter group—remember those? That the group was ostensibly "therapy" allowed me to rationalize the only intimacy I got once a week during those lonely months after my divorce. For some time afterward, I was a group junkie—what I got from and gave to others in those groups wasn't friendship, although it felt that way at the time. They were people I encountered at a crossroads in my life. When I see them now, as I occasionally do, I feel a funny kind of embarrassment as well as a sadness that we never connected on any level other than shared pain. I realize that while we have seen each other emotionally naked, that doesn't mean we are friends, and remember a story that Kay, whom I've known since college, told me.

Kay and Grania were newspaper colleagues and close friends. They were similiar in style and temperament, both highly visible, not only in their professional world but in the community. They were active in the women's movement and were perceived as independent and successful. In her private life Grania was involved with a man who was abusive to her. According to Kay, "She was a strong feminist who was in an extremely bad relationship that no one could understand—including her."

When Grania's lover left her she had a nervous breakdown. She attempted suicide; sheerly by chance Kay found her in time. Kay took her to the hospital, stayed with her while her stomach was pumped out, and moved into her home and cared for her for several days afterward. When Grania had recovered, she took a leave of absence from her job and went to Europe. When she returned, she didn't call Kay—she ignored Kay's attempts to contact her. "She simply dropped me—not just dropped me, but went after me with a vendetta," Kay told me. "She spread stories about me at the paper that weren't true; she tried to ruin my relationship with my lover; she blackballed me at the women's forum. I was deeply hurt—I've broken up with major love relationships with less pain than she caused me. We went through a period of several years of not speaking, until finally, several months ago, we happened to be seated next to each other on a plane. By then I'd decided she was potentially very dangerous to me—I'd given up trying to resolve the relationship, I just wanted to avoid her. But it was a long trip on a small plane. After an icy politeness that lasted for an hour or so, she turned to me and said, "I'm really sorry about what happened between us. I don't have any excuses; it was a very crazy time in my life." I kind of nodded—I still didn't trust her. And then she said, "I don't want to remember that time. It's like a blackness that sucks me in. I don't want to remember who I was then. And whenever I see you, it all comes back to me."

Grania's explanation "made a certain kind of perverse sense to me," said Kay. "Her apology was genuine, although to this day I don't think she really has any idea of how deeply she hurt me. Perhaps if we'd had a good mutual friendship before that—a bank of good memories and shared experiences to draw on—it wouldn't have happened. I wanted to say to her, 'Look, you can't run away from yourself. You have to accept the shadow within you, bring it into the light, to stop it controlling you.' And then I thought, *What's the use?* We'd just get back into that unequal relationship again, and I don't need that. Plus, I still don't trust her."

Trust is the difference between intimacy and friendship. According to psychologist Shirley Luthman, "In an intimate relationship, we trust each is giving freely whatever we are capable of giving, based on our abilities, limitations, and the emotional state we are in at the time. We trust each other for the gift and commitment to contact. We both trust we can spontaneously come out at any time with anything we feel and there will be room for error. We trust we will listen and not judge each other's feelings. We trust that each is committed to his own growth."[1]

All friendships do not share this quality of trust. Yet they are central and necessary to a connected life. As Marv Thomas says, we hire professionals to do many things for us that in earlier times, neighbors and friends did for each other. We exchange money for time, support, and skill sharing, functions that the personal village, clan, and community performed for each of its members. Money frees us of the obligation of reciprocity, limits the duration and extent of our commitment. The barter economy that served when we were younger and poorer no longer suffices; it's easier to hire someone to do a job than to ask a friend for help, and more reliable, too, we think, which masks the uncertainty we feel about how good a friend someone really is. Unless it's a crisis; then we feel freer to ask for what we need, which often isn't just a job to be done, but the caring, sharing, and connection we really seek.

When a friend, or even an acquaintance, is in crisis, we rise to the occasion. In fact, it may be easier to be a friend under conditions of adversity than it is when the sun is shining. Roles are defined—one hurts, the other helps—and so is duration, until the crisis is resolved, one way or another. Helping or being helped at a time like this can strengthen a relationship, increase a nonintimate connection to a closer one. Or it can hurt, as it did with Kay and Grania. Writer Jane Howard defines what close friends who truly trust can be when she says, "We are all caseload and caseworker to one another." We try to be—but some times, it backfires.

Growth demands relatedness—the most intimate friendships we have affirm and strengthen our inner selves, while others, which may be mutually useful but do not connote the level of acceptance we expect from those closest to us, may confirm, consolidate, or improve our outer selves or circumstances.

Sociologist Graham Allan defined friendship as the social exchange of love, status, services, goods, money, and information, and said that it has instrumental as well as emotional rewards.[2] Despite the current emphasis on networking as a way for women to create our own versions of the locker room where men for years have traded professional favors and connections, few women are comfortable "calling people who use each other's friends— even if it's mutual," as Cookie, an editor, says. Yet when I ask her to tell me about how her closest friendships began, most of them did, in fact, have a component of exchange. We all want something from our friends, though what we want, and what we get, differs at various stages in our relationship with them. Community and attachment, friendship and intimacy, are different—what one can provide, the other sometimes cannot, but without either we are lonely.

Friendship can be based on many things: a sharing of life-style or structure, a colleagueship related to work or other mutual interests, a joint preference for certain kinds of activities, a history of years spent knowing, if not always being together. Judith Viorst, writing in *Necessary Losses*,[3] distinguishes between: convenience friends, which involve mutual reciprocity (the social exchange theory); special interest friends, who are involved but not intimate, who *do* together rather than *be* together; historical friends, who are part of each other's pasts; crossroads friends, who were close at a particular time in the past; cross-generational friends, where the friendship has little risk or investment; and close friends, with whom we are involved in a deeply intimate relationship. Marv Thomas offers other categories, such as familiar strangers who reinforce our sense of place, of belonging to a milieu or community; the teller in the bank who asks if you enjoyed your vacation; the waiter at your favorite restaurant who notices your new haircut; coteries—members of a group who share common ground or goals and agree to support each other, such as a management quality-control circle, a women's soccer team, a co-op board; and confidantes, that inner circle that comprises family and intimate friends. Yet, as Letty Pogrebin writes, "Friendship is a category each of us invents,"[4] and we invent it according to our fears and our abilities.

LETTING YOURSELF OUT
The fears connected with friendship are these: fear of engulfment, fear of rejection, fear of abandonment, or fear of betrayal. Fears come from Small Mind's emotional recreation of an event in your past: someone whose personal boundaries, perhaps, were more or less stringent than your own; who let you down once in a crunch; who used or abused you. Janet was my best friend until seventh grade, when she discovered boys. After that, I hardly ever saw her, which is why I didn't make another close girlfriend until college. Stan was my close friend after my divorce, when I really needed a man to shore up my shaky self-image as a woman, but when I was back on my feet, he abandoned me, and it took a long time to realize that that was the only way he could relate to women—when they were down.

Sometimes the scripts we live in our friendships come straight out of childhood: "She's just using you" is one common message, and "He's only out for sex" is another. In some families, like Peggy's, friends are not considered to have as much intrinsic value as other things, like achievement, perseverance, or self-sufficiency. In others, they are not to be trusted as much as blood kin. And in almost every Sleeping Beauty's childhood, at least one of the following messages was transmitted: *Your husband will be your best friend. Grown-ups can stand on their own two feet. Friends are fine, but don't let them distract you from what really matters.*

Try to recall how Small Mind feels about friendship, even if you can't immediately connect the feeling with an event. Are you fearful or eager when you meet someone new? Do you expect people to like you, or do you feel you have to "charm" them? Do you think soul mates either recognize each other across a crowded room or grow through shared experience and risk? Are you worried that a friend will "take you over" or simply abandon you without warning? Are you possessive about your friends—do you demand exclusivity in order to feel that you matter?

TRUE FRIENDSHIP NEVER RUNS SMOOTH

One of my closest friends is a woman with a great gift for connection. "When Rita shines her light on you, it's like no one else even exists," someone once said. "You feel incredibly special, like you are the flame and she is the moth." Our friendship was fast, intense, and exciting, like a love affair. When, a few months after we met, I watched her turn her light on someone else, I felt extremely jealous. And then I began to pick at our friendship, like a scab. When she offered advice, I rejected it out of hand; I remember one conversation in which she said, as she often did, "If you want my opinion . . ." And I said, abruptly, "No, as a matter of fact, I don't."

I struggled for integrity in that friendship—to hold onto myself and to honor her—for many years. We moved through the stages that Marv Thomas identifies as benchmarks of a relationship. The stages—interest, exploration, hope, struggle, creation—came into play and to some extent flowed in and out of the space between and around us throughout the life of our friendship. We could have stopped at any stage, but we were committed to seeing it through. Our differences were apparent from the start, yet we continued to explore until we saw the possibilities for a truly intimate friendship. Somewhere around that time hope crept in, and we both began to idealize our views of our relationship; we thought we would always be together, always in synch, always in each other's lives, even though it was clear that we had different agendas and different dreams. "Hope is a projection of what we long for in the future," says Marv Thomas. "Interest becomes hope when we project it forward toward what we wish would happen. Interest is that genuine fascination with or curiousity about another person."

In those early stages, Rita and I were both on our best behavior, and that engendered an openheartedness that lasted until we tired of the effort and began to be who we really were. Sleeping Beauties don't like to struggle with relationships; they feel entitled to smooth, effortless connection, a numinous experience in which there are no hard edges, just a romantic glow of that same diffused relatedness which is supposed to be characteristic of our gender. This, after all, is where our true talents are supposed to reside: in our gift of relationship. And when we are passive rather than active in a friendship, when we react instead of acting, when we subsume our identity in the desire to merge, we sacrifice the equality and autonomy that is necessary to friendship, just as it is to intimacy. Connections must be made out of separateness, between people who are dependent on themselves for emotional survival.

The struggle and creation of real friendship demands agreement on context, and development of respect for each other's individuality. Telling Rita I didn't want her advice was a way to define boundaries. Now there are areas in which I do seek her counsel; now we have ways of testing, and respecting boundaries. In the first fine careless rapture of a developing friendship, we tend to see the other as a reflection of ourselves—we minimize differences, and in so doing often tread on the other's integrity. In struggle, we retreat to nurse our disappointment that the other turned out to be different from, not exactly like us. Sometimes we come out of this separateness and sometimes we don't. When we are midway to maturity we believe idealistically that underneath, all people are alike. Once we're really there, we understand that they are not, which is a kind of loss of innocence. But by then we feel secure enough in our own identity that we are not threatened by another's differences. One can know a friend well over a long period of time, and then be surprised when something he or she does or says reveals a sudden stranger. *Why, she's not like me after all,* we think, and are disappointed as we feel our separateness. The Sleeping Beauty self that dissolves in relationship, the "soluble self" that theologian Catherine Keller discusses in *From a Broken*

Web, "cannot differentiate loved individuals from herself . . . and lives only in the hopelessly charged intensities of the personal . . . the political, intellectual, and spiritual possibilities of relation fade."[5] Not to mention the comfort of having someone with whom you can go to trashy movies, henna your hair, and argue about—or even explain—deconstructionism.

The struggle stage of relationships leads to establishing a sense of security with each other. This is trust built over a period of time—trust that we can feel safe, will not be hurt, or embarrassed, or used. There were times in my friendship with Rita when each of us felt unsure about this. It still happens, we still test each other in our own ways and only talk about it later, when we can look back at our history and say, "I was really worried then, but you came through." Or didn't—and we talk about that, too. Perhaps the greatest test was when I wrote a novel in which a woman with many of Rita's personal characteristics was a central figure. "Why, you made me the bitch!" she said. I replied, "She's not *all* you, and besides, she's not the bitch, she's the most autonomous, independent woman in the book."

"That's what I mean—the bitch," Rita laughed. "You have permission to use my life, my relationships, everything but my name in the book, with one condition."

"Yes?" I asked, wondering how much I was going to have to rewrite.

"When they make the novel into a movie, Candice Bergen has to play me," she said.

Rita and I have moved into different worlds now. Without proximity, friendship is problematic, and often relegated to historical or crossroads categories, but often when I feel lonely, I invite Rita into my heart for a good long talk and regret that she is some four thousand miles distant. In an increasingly mobile world, we are hesitant to make the commitment to friendship, yet if we do not, we will have no guests in our aloneness as well as no companions in our connectedness. When we hold onto the specific shape or form of our fantasy of what a friend is, we ignore the possibilities for connection that are all around us. When we wait until all our fears have been allayed—of engulfment, rejection, abandonment, and betrayal—we are never really receptive to friendship; we are impenetrable, inert, rigid. When we risk the worst thing that could happen—whichever fear is foremost in Small Mind—we are alive to possibility, receptive to excitability, and vitally responsive.

THE RIGHT FRIEND FOR THE RIGHT REASON

In every woman's life there are times when any friend won't do—you need the right one. Marcia is great for helpful advice, whether it's a problem with your boss, another friend, or even how to spend your Christmas bonus. But you can't talk to her about your lover; she's all wrong when it comes to men, still bitter after a divorce, always painting the worst-case scenario. Carol, on the other hand, is invariably warm, supportive, and understanding when you're having problems in your relationship. (And when your man does something lousy and you tell her about it, and later you kiss and make up, she never reminds you of the names you called him before.)

It's easy to talk to Kathleen about your kids. She doesn't have any, but she has an objectivity you lack, and she never implies, in any way, shape, or form, that you're not a perfect mother. Margaret, who does have children, always sounds judgmental and critical when you tell her your daughter is being a total bitch or your son is flunking in school. So of course you only tell her when Jenny's hormones have quieted down and when Cam gets straight A's.

Barbara is married, so you don't ask her to go bar-hopping with you on Saturday night, but Lee isn't, and besides, she's always up for a good time. Sean wouldn't be thrilled to pick you up at the airport at midnight, but if you got in a car accident at one A.M., he'd be there in a flash. And Judy you could call at four in the morning, just because you were lonely, miserable, and afflicted with a raging case of the compulsive Milky Ways.

The point of all this, of course, is that different friends are useful and important for different reasons, at different times. Which is why it's important not to narrow your world so that only one person is available, and only in specific circumstances, to satisfy all your needs for caring, companionship, diversion, entertainment, or connection.

Many women expect a lover, partner, or husband, when they find him, to fill all their needs. Yet the partnership itself may obviate against this, especially if whatever is on a woman's mind disturbs the status quo or threatens the stability of the relationship, or alters the way in which either is viewed by the other. According to sociologist Pepper Schwartz, "Friendships outside of marriage meet key needs for both partners, and ease the pressure on the relationship to live up to impossible expectations. People in long-term dyads need friends."

Yes, but not as much as those who aren't, you think, remembering what happened when your closest friend got married or began cohabiting. There's no getting around it—when that happens, the friendship changes. Sometimes it's not so bad, especially when you truly like your friend's partner, and he or she likes you. When the relationship is a good one, it expands to include you, and although you may mourn the special closeness that isn't as available to you as it once was, you have two friends now. Even if you're a born cynic, their happiness reinforces your faith in love—the triumph of hope over experience, as Ben Johnson said.

But sometimes it's dreadful, especially when your friends seem to emphasize their bliss with a bad case of the Smugs that brings out all your insecurities, makes even the happiest, most satisfying single life feel like a dress that's been marked down from $500 to $19.95. Gerry Hirshey, writing in *The Washington Post Magazine,* says of these "coupleniks" that "They tend to 'dialogue' for hours on all details of their coupleness ... Willy-nilly, they toss their We's and their I's into conversational bouillabaisse. They're always congratulating themselves on their Subaru good sense and thanking God they're not single." And the worst of them, says Hirshey, tell jokes like this: "*Question:* How does a single woman get rid of roaches in her apartment? *Answer:* She asks them for a commitment."[6]

Like Hirshey, my editor friend Cookie has been tempted to bend, or even break the truth barrier when Mr. and Mrs. Smug trill duets about coupleness and demand to know why she, too, isn't someone's better half. "I make all my past relationships—even the ones that only lasted a weekend—into Major Affairs. I have an inexhaustible fund of Lost Loves. It's easier than telling the truth: either that I don't want to, or nobody decent has asked me lately. Both of which statements are true, I think. See? Don't get me started!" Once Cookie told a man, on their first date, that she was a widow. A few times she's implied to other people that she's been divorced. "Somehow that seems more acceptable than saying I've never been married, although I hate myself when I do it."

Every single woman who's ever had a case of gender self-hatred, however temporary, can understand Cookie's pain. It is an extreme overadaptation to the Tyranny of Coupleniks and the myth that singles are pitiable and only unpartnered because nobody wants them. Rachel Kranz, writing in the periodical *Utne Reader*, discusses her response to this:

> The problem of being single: to see my life as complete and worthwhile in itself. To take it seriously *now*, not to say, either with relief or with despair, "Well, I can't do anything about that until I find a man." I begin to see how much the term "single woman" erases. Where is the corresponding image of "unemployed woman," or "woman without a vocation"? What about "friendless married woman," or "woman with male lover but no other intimate adult ties"?[7]

Kranz realized she'd been using the image of "single woman" to defer a lot of decisions:

Should I fix up my apartment? Why bother—I'd be moving in with someone else some day. Was I earning enough money for the future? But surely my mythical partner would take care of my retirement and help me support my parents. Did I want to have children? Don't even *think* about that one. How many options had I never even considered, because finding a man would make them unnecessary? Had I ever even thought of living with a roommate, preparing for retirement, buying an apartment, exploring single motherhood? Maybe most important, how actively was I building the network of friends and colleagues that I wanted—the relationships I needed right now?[8]

Sleeping Beauties often believe that only romantic partnership can provide significant emotional ties, and discount their relationships with friends. "What about friends?" asks Kranz.

Well, no. If coupled they weren't available, if single they'd disappear as soon as *they* found men. I certainly recognized this anxiety, too. So I decided to make a radical assumption: I was never going to meet a man who would become my life-time partner.

This decision sent shock waves through her life.

At first it sounded like giving up. . . . I'm not committed to being single in the sense of actively avoiding relationships. What I'm committed to is living as though *this* life is real. The relationships that are in my life now—with myself, my friends, my work—are as real and serious as any relationship I might have someday with a partner.

As this writer began to build her emotional life around her relationships with her friends, she accepted that "it was never going to be the same as my romanticized idea of a love relationship, never going to offer the same extent of involvement, and never going to make the same extensive demands." Yet, by allowing herself to depend on her friendships, she writes, "I'm hacking out a small, temporary space beneath an imminent landslide. The negative possibilities seem so much more real to me now— and so much more painful." Friends move out of the city and she wonders if they are still primary people in her life, and whether she was foolish to think they ever were. A close friend faces a death in her family: "How much support should I offer? How much do I want to offer?"[9]

With the most intimate friends, that question answers itself. With others, it never arises. Friends are a bulwark against loneliness, "a palpable resource," and a creative, life-enhancing connection with our deepest selves as well as with each other.

LETTING GO AND TAKING HOLD
Sometimes old friendships fade and wither, or are pinched back because they demand more than we want to give, because we have changed in ways they can't accept, or because they have. Detached for whatever reason, we feel an empty place where that relationship was, like the phantom pain of a missing piece of ourselves. If there are too many other demands on our time, we put off making new friends, or following up a likely prospect, telling ourselves we can barely take care of the friends we have.

A woman quoted in Letty Pogrebin's *Among Friends* defines a friend as "someone who doesn't call me."[10] That's probably the woman whose Filofax contains scheduled appointments for sex— if you're that busy, that's fine, but who are you going to celebrate with when the project's completed, the job is over, or there's white space on your calendar? We all have different ideas about what "enough" is in relation to friendship. But if you've put all your energy into one or two friends who, for one reason or another, fall by the wayside, what do you do then?

If you're Sleeping Beauty, you wait until someone fights his or her way through your thicket of busyness, and demands to be seen. Or you sleep on in your castle, passive and inert, waiting for a friend to discover you. If you're out in the world you never talk to strangers, and if you don't have a companion, you don't go out at all. At work you suspect every offer of friendship—who is this person, and what does she want from me?—and avoid sharing your personal life with anyone because it's "unprofessional." If you join a group trip, you'll always pay the supplement for single occupancy, to save you from being stuck with someone you probably won't like anyway—if they're worth knowing, you figure, they've already got a friend to travel with. If your parents live nearby, you go home every weekend. And you're always available when your sister-in-law needs a baby-sitter at the last minute. If you're a Sleeping Beauty, you watch a lot of television, and think your favorite series characters are your friends.

There are some clear, easy-to-follow directions about finding friends, as long as you let go of a specific fantasy about what a friend should be—what sex, what age, what color, what class, what "type." The first one is that you go where people are. The second is that you talk to them. The third is that you listen when they talk back. And the fourth is that you make a decision to know them better. Somewhere on the planet—probably within a mile of where you are right now—there is someone who will enlarge your world with the simple, invaluable gift of friendship, if you have the price, which is just this: your active, receptive, available, adequate self.

LOVE IS A SOMETIME THING
If friendship is easy to find, love is slightly harder. I'm not talking about the romantic connection with a mate who may be your life partner; I'm talking about that affinity, that mutual caring and accepting, that wholehearted feeling of being important in someone's life, and that trust and commitment, that can only grow in a well-tended friendship garden. Every person you meet, know, befriend, or are befriended by, is not going to be someone you love, or who loves you. "What flows between us, even when we're

apart, is more than friendship," says Cynthia of her relationship with Dee. "We will be there for each other always. One of us will bury the other. And the one who is left will grieve forever." Of Phil, her business partner, buddy, and best male friend she says the same thing. Both of those relationships, says Cynthia, define her to herself: "I am capable of loveableness, loving, and being loved." In a loving friendship, we are most wholly ourselves, and most completely at home.

RESPECTING BOUNDARIES

No matter how close the connection, how total the love between two people, each is still an individual, and each has her own limits, boundaries, and priorities. Respecting those is crucial to friendship—understanding when someone needs to withdraw from you, or even turn to someone else, for reasons that may be unknown, requires both trust that the other is not permanently shutting you out and security that the bond can withstand it. I think of a time when someone I cared deeply for was very ill— literally, at death's door. I waited at the hospital with Stu's husband, David, and Michelle, Stu's closest friend since graduate school. Only David was allowed in the intensive-care room. Much later, after the crisis had long since passed and Stu was well again, Michelle said to me, with great sadness, "I realized then that friends simply don't have the *standing* that husbands do. When Stu got married, I never really thought I'd lost her in a real way. Somehow, I still thought I came first. I wanted to push David out of there—I knew her first, I wanted to tell him, we've shared more together than you'll ever know. I realized the limits of friendship that day—and I thought, *Who will ever be there for me in that way?* Talk about necessary losses . . ." Soon after that, Michelle, who had been the center of a large group of friends and connections, moved out of town to take a new job in a city where she knew no one. "In a way, I felt that my loving web of friends was inhibiting me, lulling me into a false sense of security that someone would put me first," she told me. She met a man and married him, and they lead what, by comparison with Michelle's earlier gregarious life, is a somewhat hermetic existence. They participate in the world primarily as a couple, so closely knit that even a child, Michelle says, would be an intrusion. She stays in distant touch with Stu, and when a friend from the old days happens to be in her city and calls, she may or may not be available, depending on her husband's schedule. "All of that diffused energy I was putting into having a lot of friends is totally focused on my husband," she says. She is making a very traditional bet—that her husband can answer all the needs in her life, and that he'll be around for the rest of it.

It would be lovely to have someone—or several someones—for whom we are always the first priority, always number one. That soluble Sleeping Beauty who dissolves in relationships is a woman at high risk of depression and unhappiness when relationships fail her, as from time to time they will. She will sense others' boundaries as rejection, feel orphaned when they are distant, jealous when their attention or affections shift away from her. And she will not be able to receive what they still have to give her.

CREATING RITUALS, VALIDATING FRIENDS

We have rituals that mark life-stage transitions: birth, adolescence, attaining one's majority, marrying, dying. And we have others for holidays that celebrate our shared culture or community. We participate in most of these in the company of family and friends, but rarely do we make the friendship itself the point of ritual, remembrance, or ceremony.

Yet affirming friendship deepens and ripens it, recognizes it as a special and meaningful bond, reminds us that we matter to each other. My first Thanksgiving after I was divorced was a lonely and miserable dinner in a near-empty restaurant with only my two toddlers for company; the next year I filled my home with the friends I'd made in the year that followed, and every fourth Thursday in November thereafter I did it again, until that image of a hamster pedaling the wheel in its cage really got to me.

Friendship Is a Category You Invent Yourself

Now I take the cranberry sauce or the mashed potatoes to someone else's table, but every now and again, having satisfied my insecurities and banished the vision of the hamster, I call the people I love most and get out the turkey roaster, even if it's not Thanksgiving—just to celebrate our connectedness. I give and go to my share of birthday parties, but with my nearest and dearest, I always have a special dinner on the first day of their birthday week to praise and cherish our friendship. And all the people I know who have a special talent for friendship have their rituals, too.

Marcy spends one night at the beginning of each of the four seasons writing special, personal notes to her friends, reminding them of times and trials they've shared since the last one, and wishing their friendship another fall, another spring. Brian calls his closest pals together on the anniversary of his divorce, to thank them again for helping him through it. Bess and Leila grew up together in a small New England town. They both live in New York now, but once a year they go home to the place where they were raised and visit the cemetery where their parents are buried. It's the only time they really see each other, but it's an important one. Clea and Therese have a twice-yearly habit of cleaning out their closets together, which results in some swapping of clothes, a great deal of laughter, and then a shopping trip during which each buys the other one a special something—a scarf, a sweater— in the same color. Five women I know who lived in a commune together years ago always celebrate the summer solstice with appropriate ceremony, ritual, music, and exchange of gifts, followed by a big party to which all their other friends are invited. And Carrie and Marcia go to a spa every year, which keeps them connected even though they now live at different ends of the continent.

Sometimes it's hard to distinguish habit from ritual, but the key difference is that ritual has a component of both awareness and celebration. It is an occasion for friends to recommit themselves to friendship—feel it, speak it, praise, and honor it. It's different from family celebrations in that they've chosen rather than been pressured to participate in it, and intention rather than blood is the bond that holds them together.

Which isn't to say that family can't be friends, too, and choice rather than obligation be the connection. It is only as adults that we can truly be friends with members of our family—when we meet as equals, or the closest to it we can be, when our family roles—mother, sister, daughter, niece, aunt—may have created the bond, but cannot alone sustain and enrich it. If we marry, we may create new families. If we do not, it is even more important that those among whom we were born and raised provide that connection we need. But ultimately, as Judith Guest writes, "If people care for each other, support each other through good and bad times, and are truly committed to helping one another become autonomous human beings, isn't that the work of a family? Can the doing of the work award you the title?"[11]

One of the archetypes to which single women often relate is the orphan. Regardless of whether our parents are alive or dead, "the orphan is a metaphor for our deepest, most fundamental reality; experiences of attachment and abandonment, of expectation and deprivation, of loss and failure and of loneliness," says therapist Madonna Kolbenschlag.[12] The inner orphan lodged in Great Mind may be connected to Small Mind's memory of being left alone as an infant, or to the loss of a former lover. The orphan makes us feel unlovable, unloved, and unloving; incapable and incompetent; unconnected; powerless to contribute or take part in shaping our world; without a future that has meaning; stuck, stagnant, incapable of growth or transformation. It is our task to confront the orphan within us, who is born of mourning our necessary losses, and reclaim ourself. Bringing the orphan into our consciousness allows us to learn to be family to each other, whether through blood or intention.

❖ 6 ❖

The Man/Woman Connection

I grew up just as the twist was taking over the space formerly occupied by the fox-trot. By the time the culture and the music got to doing your own thing on the dance floor, I was pregnant, and when I did my thing, I looked like the Hindenburg blocking out the sun all over New Jersey. No matter how hip or how liberated I got to be, I could never really convince my deepest self that a woman without a man, at least when the music started, was like a fish without a bicycle. So if I want to go dancing, I have to find a man . . . I know, it's very unliberated of me, but there you have it.

There are other things I need men for, too. I need men to hang out with—I like the way they look, I like the way they smell, I like the way they say whatever comes into their heads without wondering how I'll take it. I like it that they are different from me, and different from women. I like it that they are better at abstract reasoning than I am, so they can do geometry. I like it that they read the same newspapers as I do and don't read the same novels. I like it that they understand the ways in which business is like football and are willing to translate for me. I like it that they are taller, so they can change lightbulbs without a ladder, and stronger, so they can carry my luggage up three flights of stairs. I like it that they'll always kill the spiders, even if they're just as scared as I am. Men are a field trip into a different, but parallel, universe, and while I wouldn't like to live there, it's a great place to visit. Men make me feel part of the world. And men, even when they're not my lovers, provide my sense of sexuality.

At first I didn't want to put a chapter about men in this book. After all, this is about not waiting for the Prince. For a single woman, men are just friends, and I covered friendship a few pages ago, right?

Not quite. Men are never "just" anything. To a woman, single or not, men—friends, lovers, colleagues, bosses, husbands, exes, buddies, fathers, sons, and brothers—are Something Else.

They exist, for us, in at least two dimensions: as themselves, the particular, unique individuals they are; and also as symbols. They may stand for our unmet needs, our unrealized fantasies, or our unachieved goals. When they are in our lives we judge them not just on their own merits, but on their ability, or failure, to also be what they stand for. We want them to play multiple roles in our personal dramas, validate our femininity, provide our self-esteem, mediate between us and the grownup world, pledge their undying love, and place themselves between us and our deepest, most secret fears. No wonder we say things like "There are more great women around than there are great men," (Cookie); "Women are from Venus and men are from Mars," (Judy); or "Women are the protein in my life, and men are the carbohydrates," (yours truly).

In the game of "I can be more sexist than you," women are winning hands down. Men are getting incredibly bad press these days. In fact, this book was written partly as a response to all those other books that suggest that women's only real problem is that all men are flawed. They can't commit, they won't grow up, they dance away, they fear our strength, they think with their genitals, they're obsessed with power, they won't share their feelings, they're afraid to be vulnerable . . . and on and on and on.

So what? Those things only matter to Sleeping Beauties who believe that an unflawed man—or even one they could train— could solve their problems. Not only could, but *should*, and sometimes, *must*.

The truth is, there is really only one problem a man can solve for a woman that she cannot, and even there, life is like Weight Watchers: You can always substitute something that's available for something that's not. That problem, of course, is sex. And if it's just sex you want or need—not love, not romance, not hugging or holding or anything else except the most basic unit of friction, irritability, and release—then give free rein to your sexual fantasies, and take yourself to bed. At the very least, you'll be waking up with someone you love. And if you feel inhibited or even guilty about getting yourself a good vibrator, consider Lily Tomlin's words on the subject: "At one time I felt guilty about using a cake mix instead of baking from scratch," she said in *The Search for Signs of Intelligent Life in the Universe.* "I learned to live with that. I can learn to live with this."[1]

Of course, it isn't the same thing, except on the most basic, cellular level. But when you look at it that way, it makes it easier to detach sex from all the ideas we surround it with, all the values we bring to it, all the hopes with which we endow it. And when you look at a man in that way—as a relatively sophisticated biological unit, a well-differentiated human being, an individual, a person, a man named Max who likes classical music and hates sauerkraut, who reads poetry but loves baseball, who's fun to go out with but would make a terrible partner, who beats you at Scrabble but loses at tennis—and can distinguish him from all of the roles, needs, and goals he stands for—you are part way there. You are at least on the road to filling your life with men who can play some of those roles, meet some of those needs, and help you achieve some of the goals you've been striving for.

GETTING BEYOND THE ROLE TRAP

What does a particular man stand for in your life? Dr. Judith Sills, author of *How to Stop Looking for Someone Perfect and Find Someone to Love,* distinguishes between two sets of survival needs, biological and psychological, that order a woman's search for the Other, and warns that failure to distinguish between them may influence not only how she searches, but whom she finds, selects, or is selected by. Sills terms a woman's only biologically based needs "sperm and support." Her psychological needs include the need for security in personal relationships, the need for congenial companionship, and the need for intimacy.[2]

In a later chapter, we'll take up the issue of how an independent single woman might, on her own, satisfy her desire for children. Concerning support, we've already seen how important the ability is to take care of oneself financially through one's own efforts, and we'll go into it in greater depth in the next chapter on money. If we choose to or have to, we can handle sperm and support on our own. But it is that set of psychological needs described by Dr. Sills that speaks to Sleeping Beauties, whispers the Prince's name seductively in our ear. When we listen to it, we feel annoyed. After all, shouldn't we be able to get those needs met somewhere else? Wouldn't any good, close, loving friend, even one of the same sex, do? Well, yes. And if we're self-reliant, we find friends who provide us with security, companionship, and intimacy. Often, those friends are women—who, as it happens, are by nature better than men are at meeting those relational needs anyway. But somehow it isn't enough, we still crave and desire men. However, something happens to relational needs when we look to a man to meet them. They are transformed, subtly and not so subtly. When we seek security in a relationship with a man, we also seek sexual fidelity and exclusivity. When a man is whom we choose for congenial companionship, it is not only a mutuality of interests or goals we seek, but a way to validate that we belong, as Gloria Steinem once said, we all want to have a man to stand next to on a Saturday night. As she also said, sometimes *who* the man is doesn't matter—what does is that he *is* a man. And finally, when we look for a man to provide intimacy, we often demand what we do not ask from even our very closest friends—unconditional love and acceptance, a blurring if not a total obliteration of personal boundaries. While men may also demand that unconditional love, they often define their boundaries more precisely and maintain them with greater vigilance, which is not always a bad thing; permeability, not solubility, is a property of mature intimacy.

In infancy, we first experienced our needs for security, companionship, and intimacy as a "set"—three indistinguishable strivings that went together. They were filled by our mothers, in an intense, one-on-one relationship, which was thereafter established as the context for satisfaction. As we grew older, we saw (or imagined) that our fathers met those needs for our mothers, in a similarly intense relationship. That's when the transformation of those needs began, in our inner if not our outer lives; that's when we created a male image, a husband or life partner, to embody their fulfillment, in a context that was intense, familial, and interpersonal. And all our social and psychological conditioning since then has merely served to reinforce this primal and powerful image.

In Small Mind, Big Mind, and Great Mind, our images about who men are, what they do, and what they stand for reside, interact, and are confirmed by our experience. Authority, discipline, decision-making, money, power, and control will be a man's domain, particularly if we were raised traditionally in a home where father's word was law, brothers got the biggest portion of food or attention, sons were entrusted with family honor and invested with a family's dreams of accomplishment. Instrumental (doing) skills were valued over relational (being) ones. In Big Mind we respond to our social and cultural myths about men and in Great Mind we are surrounded by metaphors that underline our male/female differences and connote nature's arrangements for the propagation of the species. And in Great Mind, too, we all carry an image, however inchoate, of God as man, unless we have been able to imagine Him in another form.

We could argue forever about how possible it is to change this kind of conditioning, transform these images, supplant these metaphors with other ones. We could even discuss whether it would be wiser right now to say, "I'm never going to get those things from a man, so I might as well just forget it and resign myself to a life where those needs are never met." My friend Barbara and I argue about it all the time. She thinks that's a defeatist attitude. I would, too, if I were counseling resignation, which, as you will see, I am most certainly not.

It may be true that you are never going to get the *whole* set of those needs met from one triple-threat Prince, but that doesn't mean you should give up and learn to live without men. That would be taking a giant step away from half the human race—the male half. And think of the possibilities you'd miss. What I am saying is that there are men out there who might not make it as a life partner, but who can satisfy some, if not all, of your needs. And just because you might not get the whole enchilada doesn't mean you should go hungry.

But first you've got to get beyond the role trap, the one that keeps you trying to turn pretty decent frogs into substandard Princes, hoping to make every relationship with a man *the* relationship, keeping you so focused on what a man stands for that you can't really see the actual man who exists. When you are conscious of who he is, rather than simply who or what he stands for, you can lessen the power of these images and metaphors to control you. You can create and exploit the opportunities—as they exist in every woman's life—to get your needs met. But first you have to separate them out, one from another, and take apart the "set."

THE FOUR MEN YOU NEED IN YOUR LIFE

I need men I can dress up and take anywhere—cruising on a friend's boat when everyone else will be coupled, to the wedding of an ex-lover, to a business dinner dance where a "date" is *de rigueur*, to social and professional events that (sadly) assume that the entire world travels by twos.

I need men for sex, because I'm a heterosexual woman. When I tell Martha, who's gay, that I'm envious because at least she's got *that* problem solved, she says, "Why do you think it's any easier for me than it is for you?" "Well, because there are so many great women around," I tell her, "and besides, women don't play sexual games with each other like men and women do." "No there aren't and yes they do," she says. "It is just as hard for a lesbian to find a sexual friend—not a major lover, not a big-time romance, just someone with whom you have a physical as well as emotional affinity—without any relationship stuff, without any role traps—as it is for a straight woman."

Sometimes our sexual needs seem somehow, well, unseemly. As Erica Abeel wrote in a "Hers" column in *The New York Times:*

> "Male sex drive, without an object of its affection, is a widely acknowledged fact of life, respectable even, catered to in the best neighborhoods. But female sex drive without an object is not nearly so acceptable . . . in fact, it is thought not to exist at all until summoned by a princely embrace. And if it does exist? Unseemly, sordid, inadmissible. Women still do not have permission to be abstractly sexual—and women themselves often withhold the permission. . . . [We often] envy the simple life of the lady firefly, who simply flashes her light to get things rolling."[3]

I need a male buddy in my life. Someone who can translate from an alien language, as my friend Sean does. Who can tell me what a man means when he says "Let's have lunch sometime"; who can explain my son to me; and to whom I can say, "If you were my lover, would you be scared by my success (or like this dress? or let a woman support you? or father a woman-friend's child? or fix me up with your law partner?)?" My friendships with male buddies are peaceful, something that's often uncharacteristic of those with men to whom I am romantically linked. And perhaps that's the nature of romance. As Linda Bird Francke writes, "A woman can't look for peace in a relationship with a man, because if she finds it, she doesn't have a man. And vice versa. The trick is to organize the war games so that the body count is minimal."[4]

More often I find peace in my friendships with gay men, because with them, there's no sexual agenda. Like many women, I sometimes think my relationships with gay men are generally less stressful and richer in certain mutualities than my heterosexual involvements. The sexual thing is usually settled at the outset, so there's more energy available for other kinds of sharing. Between a straight woman and a gay man there is a freedom from the roles and expectations that insidiously but inexorably define the behavior of a man and woman who may, or may not, come to be lovers. Certainly, a straight woman's connection with a gay man has its own problems. In the company of homosexuals, I sometimes feel irrelevant, if not invisible, and I'm sometimes called to account for unwitting sexisms and thoughtless slurs. I once remarked to my friend Jim that it was a terrible waste that a man I found attractive was gay; I didn't notice my gaffe until he replied, through clenched teeth, "For whom?"

There are women who refuse to go out with gay men; it's humiliating, says one, and another calls it pointless. You can't argue with comments like that; I know some people who still think Nixon was framed, and as long as we don't discuss politics, we manage quite well. And there are women whose only close male friends are gay, so scarred are they by previous romantic encounters; you can't argue with them, either. And there are still other women who pursue gay men and attempt to "rehabilitate" them sexually. They're often the same women whose only straight male friends are married, otherwise inappropriate, or hopelessly unable to function in an ongoing, mutually rewarding, heterosexual relationship. But in a culture that connects suppression of emotion with masculine identity, only gay men have the freedom to acknowledge that they feel. Gay men understand the language of feelings because they've been hard pressed to ignore or suppress the frequent pain of living gay in a mostly straight world. And, having discarded some culturally cued male behavior, they are freer to ignore some of its less appealing aspects and to tolerate playfulness, spontaneity, and even theatricality. Most straight men are embarrassed by such manifestations of personality; they label it childish, silly, feminine. My gay men friends do not. Often it isn't the sexual thing that makes intimacy difficult in a heterosexual union—it's the emotional thing. With straight men, I always wonder, *Where is this going?* With gay men, we're already there.

We all need men as teachers, escorts, lovers, and confidantes . . . above all, we need them as friends. If we can get one basic need met from one man, that's great. More than one is even better. But a funny thing happens with men: They don't always stay in the headings we've filed them under. Sometimes we want them to meet other needs, and they don't. Or they do, and the relationship changes—or doesn't. And sometimes the very nature of the connection, or the obligations each of us has to others, makes filling additional needs difficult or hazardous.

Joy, who always seems to be feasting on a well-balanced diet of male companionship, says of one of her friends, "Michael, who is married, is my teacher in various areas. I go to him for financial advice, for the male point of view on a particular subject, and for facts and information about which he has knowledge, like convertible debentures, real estate investment trusts, and whether short skirts are ever appropriate in the boardroom. He says they are if your legs are good enough, by the way. Michael and I have known each other forever. There are things we don't talk about—like if he should have an affair. I know he thinks about it—I also know if we talked about it, it would feel real to him, the idea of it. Also, it's as much a betrayal of his wife as his doing it would be. I don't mean with me, I mean with anyone. There's a lot of juice between Michael and me, but we don't act on it. We just flirt and enjoy it. Sometimes that's all I need from a man—just to know he finds me sexy."

For times when that isn't enough, Joy has a lover. Their relationship is sporadic and spontaneous. "He is a colleague of mine from the office. He is not married, but frankly, we don't want to be any kind of public act. Neither of us needs that. We share very little about work—because we are on the same level, and theoretically competitors, I feel limited in my freedom to tell him if I'm having any work-related problems, or even successes. But we are very, very good in bed together. And every few weeks, we end up there. I would say we are not very intimate, but we are necessary in each other's lives right now, and we are careful with each other's feelings, sensitive to nuance, even if we don't spend much time talking about it. I feel closer, for instance, to Bill, who is a buddy and a playmate, but not a lover. I can take him anywhere from a fancy dress ball to a hike in the woods. Terry, who's gay, is one of my closest male friends. In some ways he's like my brother. We give more to each other—tenderness, laughter, presents—than we do to anyone else."

As satisfied as Joy is with the variety of men in her life, she admits she'd like to be in a fulfilling relationship with one man. "I hope I will be—someday," she says. "In the meantime, I'm not sitting around waiting for the phone to ring."

MAKING FRIENDS OF LOVERS, AND VICE VERSA

Where in this hierarchy of needs, you may wonder, is romance? It may be there in that slight frisson of sexual excitement you feel when good old Bill shows up in his tuxedo, or when, at some point in a friendship, you begin to wonder whether, if reception is so good on the channels you're getting, it might be equally sharp on some others. It may be there in the sense of possibility you feel when a friend, buddy, date, or confidant indicates there's more to be had than what you originally signed up for. Or it may not be; it just may be you wishing it were, dealing with that image of the Prince again and trying to turn a nice frog into royalty. Of course, the most durable romantic relationships have a major component of friend in them—something that can take the place of awe and wonder when the rapture wears off—but not all friendships have romantic potential. He may be everything you want in a man, but he just doesn't make your pulse quicken. You may be the woman he likes above all other women, but simply not his sexual type. You may be in lust as well as in like with each other, but the timing is wrong, or there are obstacles in the way, or both of you simply prefer to live singly. Whatever your connection is with a man, it will not always, or probably even very often, be one in which the reception is terrific on every single channel. And the whole trick to having men in your life—men to go places with, to sleep with, to learn from, to confide in, to hang out with, to confirm your OK-ness as a woman—is this: *to let that be OK.* To desist from trying to bend, twist, fold, or otherwise mutilate a completely adequate human being—who happens to be male— into the Prince of your dreams or the relationship of your fantasies.

We were raised to believe that the only mature relationship with a man was in a marriage. That when we had husbands we'd be grown up. That when we were paired for eternity we'd know the secret of the universe. That love was the meaning, and without it, all else was meaningless. Sleeping Beauties still believe that. The rest of us are out having a good time.

When you make a man stand for an entire set of needs, you objectify him. He becomes not the subject of your gaze, your attention, but the object of your fantasies. In your eagerness to get your needs met, you lose sight of who he truly is. You focus on yourself rather than on him. And the friendship that might grow into love, or even someone to take to your cousin's bar mitzvah, never gets a chance to flourish.

It's not always known on first meeting a man what kind of connection will be made—how deep, how well-rounded, how enduring. When Sleeping Beauty wakes up, she begins to encounter men not only with her outer self, but with that inner, congruent awareness that Jung called the active imagination—a state of reverie in which judgment is suspended but consciousness preserved. As Dr. Sills writes, the misperception, the incongruent awareness, is that "someone else must push all your buttons and your response will be entirely out of your control. Anyone who is so helpless before that negative attitude has only one option—to wait for magic. The catch is, it can be a very long wait and the magic can be a very short ride."[5]

Many women today are truly ambivalent about how important a role they desire a man to play in their lives. They are happy and satisfied in their singleness, but are often seized by self-doubts about the course they have chosen, if conscious choice rather than a default decision is what they have truly made. Maturity is the realization that singleness, even if it doesn't seem that way, is the result of choices you have made thus far. Coming to terms with ambivalence about your feelings and your situation is a benchmark of maturity. It is not about whether you made the best choice of life-styles thus far, but the better one. And if you want to make a different choice, you can. You may be single and anxious—not because you feel miserable without a man, but because you don't. You may not feel at all ambivalent about your life-style now, but worried about whether you'll still be as satisfied with it later, or defensive when you feel called upon to stand up for it. And your confidence in your own femininity may take a beating as a result.

Arlene, who ended a satisfying relationship with Rob because he was ready for marriage and she wasn't, now wonders if she did the right thing. "My life is arranged the way I want it," she says. "I loved Rob a great deal. I simply didn't want to marry, and that was the only way I could keep him. I wanted the freedom to live my life as I chose to. I have that now, and it's very satisfying. But I wonder how I'll feel ten years from now." And Ellie, who feels like a failure because she is single, though self-sufficient and the center of a life filled with friends and pleasures, is only beginning to understand that she need not give up the idea of marriage as a goal, just of marriage as a measurement of how mature, feminine, and successful she is.

The more options for relating to men that exist in a woman's life, the less marriage or life partnership appears to be the only satisfying connection. A single woman's life offers a wide array of options; the more numerous your choices, the more hesitant you may be to commit to only one, especially one that rules out so many others. "When I was married, every day was the same," says

Carrie. "Now that I'm not, every day is a new possibility. Would I marry again? Yes, if the right man appears. But meanwhile, I'm enjoying the possibilities."

The sources of well-being in a single woman's life are not unreachable, but within her own control. Some of those sources are relational, pleasure rather than work-oriented, and involve the fulfillment of basic psychological needs—by one man or many. You can develop your own sources instead of waiting for a fantasy Prince to provide them.

A BALANCED DIET OF RELATIONSHIPS AND COMMITMENTS

All of women's psychological needs are not a "set," and all are not best satisfied by marriage. Specific, practical, workable commitments that avoid the role trap, that are changed only by mutual consent, and that are tied to what is realistically possible, given the abilities and maturity of both persons involved, can give unmarried relationships much of the security that is supposed to but does not always come with marriage.

Meaningful relationships can exist in a context of your own creating, or cocreating. They may not look like marriage, and may in fact not be anything like marriage; still, while they last they provide emotional security, congenial companionship, and intimacy. And when they're finished, there is no feeling of failure lingering like a bitter taste on the tongue.

The independent woman is dependent for emotional survival on herself. She takes responsibility in any relationship with a man for her own satisfaction, her own happiness, and her own desires. She doesn't project them onto an idealized fantasy who must stand for someone other than who he actually is.

THE DIFFERENCE BETWEEN WANTING AND WAITING

You may in fact be looking for a mate. And if you've looked for a long time, you may be telling yourself, or listening to others tell you, that the best way to find one is to give up looking for it. "It's that old sixties Zen stuff about turning your back so opportunity can tap you on the shoulder," says my friend Karen. Dr. Judith Sills puts it this way:

> The superstition that only those people who don't want a mate, who are essentially busy doing other things, will find one is just that—a superstition. There is a useful purpose to this folk wisdom; it is a way of advising people to relax about their feelings. It revolves around the idea that no one wants to present a public image of weakness or desperation. . . . It urges people to deny what they are seeking in the magical hope that it will suddenly appear. It forces you to look . . . behind your own back. And if you cannot acknowledge that you are seeking something, how do you know when you've found it?[6]

In her practical, no-nonsense guide for the woman who is seeking a mate, Dr. Sills advises clarifying what you are looking for, and learning to recognize what someone else has to offer. These are the same strategies that women who aren't looking for lifetime partners, but still want men in their lives in basic and significant ways, would do well to emulate. Acknowledgment is the bridge between wanting and waiting.

WHEN THE AFFAIR IS OVER

We all make choices about love based on past relationships, current life structures, and ongoing commitments to ourselves and others. The end of a long-term relationship may usher in a period of contentment with singleness—relief from ambivalence or emotional pain, rediscovery of one's inner self and the resources that exist to nurture it, freedom from focusing on meeting someone else's needs. The end of a marriage or a long-term affair is a chance to explore the possibilities of being alone. This can be satisfying to a woman for a long time. But then the moment arises when psychological needs resurface, and you catch yourself gazing at the handsome stranger who passes you on the street, or looking at a man you already know in a whole new way. Suddenly you realize you're available again . . . or even, perhaps, for the first time. If you can separate your needs and see the men in your life as capable of meeting some, rather than all of them—if you let those men be who they are, rather than who they stand for—you won't stop looking for the one you'd like to share your life with. And you won't be so needy, so desperate, that when you find him, you scare him away.

At a time like this, even good friends, a challenging career, satisfaction with solitude, a balance of interests and activities that stimulate and engage your mind, body, and spirit may all not seem adequate enough to overcome those feelings of romantic longing. But without them, you are much more prone to anxiety, depression, and loneliness. Without them, you are Sleeping Beauty again, back on your couch in the castle, suspended in time that passes whether you notice or not . . . waiting.

FRANNIE—"I ASK A LITTLE FROM A LOT"

I went to visit Frannie one weekend when I was feeling low about men. It seemed like years since I'd had what could remotely be called a date. Actually, it had only been a couple of months, but during the interim I'd surveyed the possibilities, and the picture wasn't rosy. There wasn't a decent man within miles—or if there was, I hadn't met him.

Frannie was having a party. "Will there be any men coming?" I asked hopefully. "A few," she replied, so I put on an extra coat of mascara. Later I said, "A few? There were more attractive, available, interesting men at your party than I've ever seen under one roof!" I was still reeling from the shock. "Maybe I ought to move to San Diego," I told her. "Give up my house, my job, my friends . . . sure, why not?" "Calm down," Frannie said. "They all have a fatal flaw."

While we washed the dishes and emptied the ashtrays, she filled me in on the dirt. They were men she'd dated, met through other friends, or knew from her work. And all the women were close friends. Some of them had been involved with one or another of the male guests at one time, so the fatal flaws Frannie recounted were occasionally based on secondhand knowledge.

They weren't fatal enough to impress me—there was hardly an axe-murderer or child molester in the lot. But Frannie's style, needs, and standards are different from mine. What she knew about the men simply added up to the fact that none of those present was quite what she wanted. Still, there was real warmth and camaraderie in the way she related to them, and they to her. In fact, she was connected to the men in that room in real, vital, and caring ways. Two of them were ex-lovers, and one was a man who cared for her during a long illness some years ago.

"I'm in that middle ground right now. I wouldn't say I'm desperate for a relationship, but if the right man came along, I'd certainly give it some thought," Frannie said. "So I get a little from a lot. I don't ask for everything from one guy. I haven't met one I'd want to give everything to. That could happen, I suppose. Meanwhile, I'm having fun with good enough guys. Not perfect ones, but I'm not perfect either. See, I'm not consistent. One day I want to be totally wrapped up in one man, and the next, I notice that he picks his teeth after he eats. There hasn't been one in a long time where I wouldn't care if he did."

Frannie is thirty-five, and has never been married. "I notice I'm evaluating men differently now," she said. "I'm starting to think about having children, so one of the first things I do when I meet someone is wonder how he'd be as a father. I dated one man for six months because he seemed genetically perfect, plus financially comfortable, interested in having kids, and available. It was like, I knew I could get what I wanted from him—a baby. I really tried to fall in love with him. He asked me to marry him, and I realized, this is all this guy could do for me, and that's not enough. He would be a terrific daddy, but an incredibly boring husband. You know the guy who Roxy, the secretary on L.A. Law, married on the show? The short, bald direct-mail mogul? Well, Charley was just like him. My mother said, 'Frannie, you're nuts. Look at what you're giving up.' My sister said, 'So marry him, have a kid, and get a divorce. Also a good settlement.' I'm ashamed to say I almost did."

Frannie has a current lover, but she doesn't see that relationship going anywhere either in the near future, except to bed. "He's the confirmed bachelor, and I can see why," she said. "He really prefers to be alone most of the time. It's a big deal for him to stay the whole night after we make love. He has a lot of boundaries, most of which I kept tripping over when we first started seeing each other. Now I've recognized them, and tried to respect them. When we're together, it's very fulfilling for me—he's really there, you know? But then *splat*, that's it, until the next time. Nothing in between. No dailyness. I couldn't change him if I tried. But he doesn't sleep with anyone else. We're exclusive that way, by mutual agreement, until one of us wants to change it. Not because of undying love, but for health reasons. We both were tested for AIDS before we had sex. If I met a man I wanted to sleep with now I'd ask him to do that for me, the way Geoff asked me. At first I was insulted, but then I understood it just makes sense. You don't have to go without sex if you're single, but you have to be sure it's safe. Because what if you met someone you really loved, and gave it to him—or vice versa?"

"But aren't you just settling?" I asked. "Don't you really rationalize this because underneath, you keep hoping he'll change?" Frannie shook her head.

"No," she said. "First of all, I know he won't. And even if he did I couldn't live with someone that unsocial, that introverted. I couldn't get him to come here tonight, you notice. Crowds make him crazy, and to him, twelve people is a crowd. In some ways he is a very selfish person. He had a vasectomy a few years ago, so children are out, too. Plus, he hates to travel, and he doesn't like to do much of what matters to me. On the other hand, he's a great lover, he's thoughtful about little things, and he's really open about his feelings. I don't see myself as settling. I still feel available where other guys are concerned. I'm still looking. And sometimes I'm lonely and depressed. But a little loneliness is part of being responsible for yourself."

Frannie has a male mentor at the office, a slightly older man who has helped her advance through the corporation, with whom there is no sexual agenda and little connection outside of the office. "George takes my ambition seriously, and gets his own payoffs, personally and professionally, from his relationship with me. I'm his line into middle management—he says he gets a sense from me of what people's strengths and weaknesses are. And on another level, I'm like a student—he enjoys teaching me, using his knowledge to help me grow. I have learned a great deal about the practically all-male world of the corporation from him. He is one of the most important men in my life. I don't bring my romantic problems to him—he'd be useless there, and probably embarrassed, too. But I've got other men in my life for that."

The man Frannie brings those problems to is an ex-lover. "It was years ago—one of those relationships that flared up and burned very brightly for a few months, and then it was over. He broke it up, and I was devastated for a while. But I have managed to keep him as a friend—I have never been a door-closer. And because he knows what I'm like in a relationship, he's really good to talk to when I'm having problems with another man."

Frannie has a couple of married men she considers important connections in her life, too. One is her partner in a small real estate investment deal, and another is her lawyer. "In both cases, we recognized when we met that there was this spark between us. And it is still there. We also recognize that we're never going to act on it. Frankly, their principles are stronger than mine—I've had affairs with married men. One lasted almost six years. It ended when he started having other problems in his life—with his job, with his kids. I really cared for him, but I finally said, 'It seems like I'm just one more problem to you. I make you feel guilty, and you don't need that. So why don't we just stop this?' And we did. He was my only sexual partner then, and I missed him. But that's the benefit of being the Other Woman—I didn't feel that I had to deal with his personal angst. I could choose not to be part of it."

COULD YOU BE THE OTHER WOMAN?

There are many women today who find relationships with married men acceptable. It is, in fact, a new social pattern, judging by the statistics. It results partly from the demographics—supply and demand—and also from the changing patterns of women's lives, women like Frannie, who, at the time of her involvement with a married lover, did not want to marry. For one thing, her fast-track job demanded most of her time and energy, and what was left was filled with friends, interests, and other commitments. She was autonomous and independent, and "not looking for trouble when I found it." But when she met Pat she was immediately attracted to him, and the feeling was mutual. She had been celibate for a long time; he told her he had had one other affair during his marriage. "He made no apologies," said Frannie. "He didn't tell me his wife didn't understand him. He never led me to believe, in any way, that he would leave her. And I never hoped that he would. Our affair was predictable—I knew when I would see him— Monday after work, and Thursday evenings. That didn't change, even when his wife went out of town—we never took advantage of opportunities like that, never looked for them. So I didn't spend a lot of hours wishing for him when I knew it wasn't possible. I never even considered him on Christmas or other holidays. We were very discreet—his wife never found out, and even my best friends didn't know. As a matter of fact, that heightened the sexiness rather than made me feel cheap. He was a very safe relationship for me. He met my sexual needs, and he never made demands on me. I did the same for him."

There are women who would never consider having affairs with married men, and there are women who would, and do. Like Linda, who says she blundered into her first encounter with a married man. "I wasn't looking for it, neither was he, but we had this intense energy around our relationship on a project we were doing together, and it ignited the sexual attraction between us. It didn't last long, but it made me start considering certain kinds of married men as being available for what for me was a relationship with definite advantage. I don't have room in my life for a daily, demanding relationship, but I have needs for warmth and sex and caring. With a married lover, I don't experience conflicts between work and love, and I'm not horny anymore."

Once you've been in a relationship with a married man, you learn to interpret the signals they give you, the cues. If you don't rule it out from the get-go, you learn to give the right ones back. And then you assess whether this is something you both can manage without overwhelming guilt or other kinds of psychic damage. Says Linda, "I don't sleep with married men I think will fall in love with me, or toward whom I feel too emotionally vulnerable. But I don't rule out a man just because he's married, either. In a relationship with a married man, I'm in control. Right now, I need that. Maybe at another time, I won't. There have been times when I only wanted sex with intense, total emotional intimacy. Usually it was when I wanted that to make up for a lot of other things I was lacking. I wanted to throw myself into a relationship because the rest of my life was lousy. Now I take sex where I can find it. It really surprised me to learn that it could be satisfying that way."

Women who have been married to and divorced from unfaithful husbands are the most dead set against affairs with married men, which is not surprising. They have been known to drop even their best friends when they learn that they are involved in such affairs. And you may not find many of your women friends, married or single, offering sympathy when your relationship makes you crazy, as it eventually may. When Frannie told me about her affair with Pat, she wasn't asking for my moral judgment, and I wasn't offering it. What she did provide, however, was her own rule of thumb regarding Other Womanhood: "Once it's a passion, twice it's a pastime, three times it's a pattern. And you know what you do with a pattern, don't you? Cut it out."

THE TRANSITION MAN

Sometimes a woman needs a man to help her recover from the last one. A man who will restore her self-esteem, her sexual confidence, her zest for life, or her feeling of wholeness. This is particularly true for women who have been recently divorced. Many Sleeping Beauties tend to confuse the transition man with the Prince. They see in him all the attributes that were lacking, or leaked out of, the recently departed Other. They invest him with all the needs unmet in the previous relationship. They often confuse the rebuilding of their sexual egos with love, the restoration of their self-image with their reflection in the transition man's eyes. Before they know it, they've made him stand, not for someone else, but for themselves. And quicker than that, they've made a commitment between two strangers; strange to each other, and, in Beauty's case, unknown to herself—because the self shattered by the failure of a relationship is not the autonomous, independent, capable, and fully conscious woman who is able to combine subjective judgment with objective detachment. She cannot distinguish passion from love, excitement from mutuality, desire from durability. She is seeking to dissolve into a relationship; she may be looking for a saviour, someone who will help her avoid facing a cold and lonely world where she'll have to fend for herself. Even if she pronounces herself satisfied with her new independence, it has a finite quality. It may have been a long time since this woman dealt with relating to men in any way except in the context of a committed relationship. Since it is the only way she remembers, she often pushes for more than she, or the relationship, can handle. In her eagerness not to be alone, she projects her fantasies onto any reasonably attractive, somewhat available, moderately OK guy. Everything is fine until he steps out of the picture she has drawn of the two of them together and demands to be seen and acknowledged for who he is—just a nice guy, looking to spend time with a nice woman.

We all carry our romantic histories into every new relationship we have. When that history is still vitally alive within us—when it is not in the past, even though the marriage or affair is over, but still painfully felt in the present—we cannot connect with another in a truly responsive way. What we respond to is not the man who shares our evening, weekend, or bed, but the one who no longer does. What we demand of our new companion is that he make up for the pain we have suffered. And what we give him, and ourselves, is heartburn.

Mark Kramer, writing in the "About Men" column of *The New York Times* says, "After a breakup I followed the patterns predicted in the grief and mourning manual. I rehearsed the trauma until I became bored by my own fury. I internalized the good relics, healed and grew cheerful again. I experienced these emotions on schedule, like some beaver building a dam." Kramer writes movingly of trying not to pin his hopes on a new love: "But things aren't back to normal, even though I am; what is not normal, for me, is being single. . . . If a key to happiness is not to want, awaiting new love eases one into paradoxical nonendeavor. The puzzle of such times has no answer; how to want, but not need." Love, he concludes, comes by chance. "The timing must be fortuitous. You can hardly articulate, much less ask for, the things that turn out to count most. . . . Love probably can't be advertised for, but it surely happens, has happened to me before. And I wish it would again, next week."[7]

Next week doesn't come until you've grieved and mourned for a lost love, healed, and grown cheerful again. What comes while you're still letting go is something else. A transition man. Useful, necessary, and, for a while at least, fulfilling. But you no longer need a man in the same way you once did. As Michael Blumenthal says in another essay from "About Men," "Women have their own homes, their own careers, their own values, their own network of women friends, their own sense of security—even, in many cases, their own children. And if indeed they 'need' men, those needs are, clearly, of a different genre. For partners, not protectors. For equals, not oppressors. For someone to look across at, not up to."[8]

The art of living single means knowing what you have to offer a man, and what he has to offer you. If you can't get past the negative attitudes about men engendered by a painful, finished relationship, you won't be looking for a mate, but trying to prove that Small Mind is right—there's no one worthwhile out there. Or you'll be turning the ones who are into men they aren't, never were, and never will be.

As Colette wrote in a story called "Bella Vista," "It is absurd to suppose that periods empty of love are blank pages in a woman's life. The truth is just the reverse. . . . When a love affair is over, there comes a lull during which one is once more aware of friends and passersby, of things constantly happening as they do in a vivid crowded dream. Once again, one is conscious of normal feelings such as fear, gaiety, and boredom; once again, time exists and one registers its flight."[9]

Between the affair and the lull, there is pain, memory, and brief wrenching bouts with desire. There is the retreat to the couch in the castle—a place to tend a broken heart. But then comes the lull, when life, if you seek it, can be a place where you and love—or at least you and a man—can meet. What happens after that is up to you.

❦ 7 ❦

If Money Could Buy Happiness, Could You Afford It?

When I was growing up, I got an allowance. My father handed it over every week, along with his customary, cautionary lecture about careful budgeting. I ignored it; I was always having to borrow against next week, and he always let me. Our running joke was that by the year 2000—"If I live that long," he used to say—I might catch up with my overdraft.

He didn't, and I never did, either. I stopped getting an allowance a girlhood ago, yet ever since then I've had this recurring fantasy about money. It arrives, in my imagination, from some unexpected source—a windfall, a lottery win, an inheritance from a distant relative I never even met, a hugely successful best seller that gets made into a Hollywood movie. It makes me rich enough so I can turn over all my money matters to the trust officer of a bank. In my imagination, he is an impeccably tailored, silver-haired, sixtyish gentleman—like the man in the Hathaway shirt ad, but without the eyepatch. He pays all my bills and takes care of all my accounts; I never have to worry about opening the mail again, because what's in it are love letters, lavish catalogs, invitations to parties—and, of course, a regular check, presumably written against dividend income, which is one of those lines on the tax return I've never had to worry about. This is my allowance, and when I overspend it—as, despite my best intentions, I occasionally do—I can always wheedle an advance out of my wise, kindly, understanding trust officer.

This is a classic Sleeping Beauty fantasy, one that occurred to me for the first time long before my father died. An analyst would say I was symbolically transferring my dependency needs onto someone who would be there even when he no longer was. It made no difference to my unconscious that I'd been self-supporting for years; the fantasy embodied my resistance to confronting the realities of my economic existence, a resistance shared by every woman who ever believed that Daddy would buy it—and if he didn't or couldn't, some other man would.

DADDY WILL BUY IT

In most middle-class families, children received allowances the way I did. And many of our mothers got them, too. So it isn't surprising that we came to believe that money derived from men, and was conditional on our compliance with whatever we were expected to do or be. If we married, we transferred those expectations to our husbands; if we didn't, we continued to fantasize about the Other who would someday fulfill them. Once we joined the labor force in large numbers, even in the professional ranks, we projected our money attitudes onto our employers; our paychecks, which came from men, or male-defined institutions, seemed like allowances, too, doled out for loyalty, dedication, perseverance, and obedience. That attitude, which is largely unconscious, often makes us discount the real meaning of a salary, which is merely the financial representation of the market value of work. It is an attitude that many employers take advantage of, especially when it comes to paying us as much as they pay men for the same work. When we know that it is our work that has value, we know that someone will always pay for it. When a paycheck is a reward, someone has the power to give it or take it away; when self-worth and financial worth are bound up together or otherwise confused, both are vulnerable, and both are constantly at risk.

Author Warren Farrell has written that men have always traded power and money for love and sex, and women have done the opposite. Even if we earned our allowances by doing household chores, the message that came with it defined money as relational rather than instrumental—as girls, we got it for being, not for doing. This distinction, which took up lodging long ago in Big Mind, is directly related to the difficulties Sleeping Beauties have as adults in dealing with money in a realistic, nonemotional way.

Dodging the financial facts of our lives by believing that someone will save us, someone *must* save us, is part of our ambivalence about money. Transferring that need to an impossible financial goal, however, is no more realistic; we then rely on money to take care of us and neglect the relationships that also nourish and support us. There is no sum great enough to rescue us from responsibility for our own lives—emotional as well as financial. And whether or not we marry, according to actuarial projections, we will outlive our husbands. We will have to secure our own future as well as our present whether we are partnered or single.

We often feel victimized by money; uncomfortable as that feeling is, it seems preferable to facing the pain entailed in taking charge of it, which is akin to the state of not being helpless, not needing to be taken care of. Money may be the most convenient place to deposit our anxieties about independence, but it is far from the safest one. While a man's symbolic interpretation of money's meaning may be power, ours is dependency. If we feel that our needs are too needy, as many women do—if we have been conditioned to judge our dependencies as immature, childish, or neurotic—we may only be able to approach them through symbols, and only act them out unconsciously.

THE SYMBOLIC MEANING OF MONEY
Recognizing that money exists for us in symbol as well as reality suggests that finding a metaphor to express those symbols may be a way to start deciphering money's cryptic meanings. Here's one

I found in my friend Mimi's medicine cabinet. (What was I doing there, you ask? What even the most morally impeccable among us does, from time to time—sneaking a peek.)

Scanning the contents of Mimi's tidy shelves was like peering into her soul. In the jars, tubes, and bottles were her fantasies, dreams, anxieties, lotions, and potions to soothe her rough edges, ease her pain, compensate for her deficiencies, regulate her emotional and sexual cycles, protect her from the ravages of age. All that, plus a new shade of lipstick I was dying to try.

I resisted the urge, and instead, I shared my money metaphor with Mimi, who is a close enough friend not to mind that I'd been peeking. Mimi loved the image, even though she doesn't need a symbol to approach what, for Sleeping Beauties, is a frightening, complex, emotion-laden subject. She can get right to the point. Dollars and cents don't give her a headache and debits and credits don't scare her. She understands money, respects it, and likes to talk about it. But she is a financial planner who realizes that many women do not. Some of us feel that money is a terrifying subject; still, we can't stop thinking about it. A few believe it's unfeminine to discuss it. Others believe it's crass. And most of us, unlike Mimi, consider it strange and mysterious, operating according to laws we don't understand and luck that always seems to happen to other people.

Somehow, money is demystified when we can find an image, a symbol, a metaphor to describe it. When Carol does this, she imagines a beach. "There is this shoreline, and the tide—money—comes in and goes out," she told me. "Every once in a while a storm washes something ashore—a tax refund check, a bonus—or takes something away—a sudden emergency that depletes my savings, a change in the economy, a financial disaster like needing a new transmission."

When Pat tries to conjure up a metaphor for money, she sees a seed packet. "Some of them will grow, and some won't," she says. For Barbara, money's image is a light bulb in a dark hallway.

"I keep stumbling, bumping into walls, and when the light goes on, I can see all the way to the end of the hall, including doors I didn't know were there."

Thinking about money metaphorically makes sense—money, after all, is only a symbol itself. It is value, expressed by a number, the invisible made visible. And it's knowing what the invisible is—what the symbol stands for, the meaning it has for you—that's the trick about money.

LIES WOMEN TELL THEMSELVES—AND EACH OTHER

We all use money for a specific purpose; sometimes we use it for all purposes, even those it can't possibly fulfill. As we once, or even still, thought a man could solve our problems, make up for what we lack, protect us against the unknown, provide us with meaning, we now often believe that money might. Dollars and cents, panaceas and palliatives—it's all the same thing, symbolically speaking. When we talk about what will keep us, what will save us, what will cure us, Sleeping Beauties who have stopped talking about men have started talking of money.

That in itself is a significant change. "Money is the last frontier of self-disclosure," says Dr. Pepper Schwartz, coauthor of *American Couples: Money, Sex, and Power.* Even a population so willing to tell all—to anyone who'll ask or listen—about the most intimate details of our lives (have you watched Phil or Oprah lately?) buttons its lip when the bottom line is mentioned.

A few years ago, with a group of women who ranged in age from twenty-five to fifty, I participated in the first honest, candid, open discussion of money I'd ever had with anyone—including my lawyer and accountant. There were fourteen of us, writers, editors, and journalists, invited by the government of Greece to see firsthand the effects of a recently enacted family code that, among other things, gave Greek women the right to own and control their own money and property. Privately, we congratulated ourselves on our good fortune in living in a country that had placed no such restrictions on our own economic freedom. "Not that we do a hell of a lot with it," said Marcia. "Except spend it," Carrie chimed in. "And pay taxes on it," Lynden added. "And worry about it," Phyllis said. "Do you think a feminist journalist can be had for the price of a room with a view of the Parthenon?" I asked. "Not had, but rented," Carrie replied. "Are we going to talk about money or not? And who's taking notes?"

I was. Someone else ordered up another bottle of ouzo, and, stimulated by the rough, licorice-tasting national beverage, we told each other exactly how we felt, what we thought, and what we did about money.

Of course, we didn't divulge exact figures—"Nobody does that," said Marcia, "which is how they keep us in our place. If we all knew how pitiful our salaries were compared to men's, or even each other's, we'd set fire to our in-baskets." Her comment touched off a lively discussion about comparable worth, which quickly degenerated into ain't-it-awfuls, which is where discussions by women about money usually begin and end. But not that night. We were debating whether women earn sixty-six or sixty-seven cents of every dollar earned by men—"trust us to quibble over pennies," said Marcia—when suddenly we noticed that Harriet was crying.

At fifty, the eldest among us, Harriet had also seemed like the calmest and wisest. She had the maps, the schedules, the details of where we were to show up on what day and at what time. She also had the sewing kit, the Band-Aids for blisters, even a flashlight in her bag, plus baby pictures of her first grandchild. Professionally, too, she was senior to most of us—she had a secure, well-paying job as editor in chief of a prestigious magazine. Harriet's tears made us all nervous, and so did her story. "I don't know what I'm going to do," she said. "I left all the money decisions to my husband, and he's about to go bankrupt. My marriage is falling apart. I just have no respect for him anymore. What kind of man can be so stupid about money? Who's going to take care of me when I'm old? My children?"

Veterans of consciousness-raising groups all, we listened and sympathized, and talked and shared, and when the sun came up and the ouzo wore off we were still at it.

"I never expected to have to pay for my own old age," said Christine, a stunning, blond, childless divorced forty-year-old Californian who once wrote a best-selling book. Christine, we thought, was the most sophisticated among us: She had great style, an inexhaustible fund of stories from the world of glitz and money her romance with fame and fortune had opened to her, and a wonderful, bawdy sense of humor. But her current financial situation was nothing to laugh about. "I earned a lot of money a few years ago, and it just sort of slipped through my fingers," she said. "The book may be the only windfall I'll ever get—my only chance to get rich. I didn't think I'd need it. I thought I'd get married again. I don't even have an IRA. I was going to open one this year, but when the time rolled around I thought, *What good is two thousand dollars going to do me when I'm sixty-five?* So I spent it on a new computer. At least with that, maybe I'll write another book."

"You should have put the money in an IRA and financed the computer. It's a business expense; you can deduct the cost, depreciate it, get a tax break on some of the interest," said Therese. I'd noticed, in the week we'd been traveling together, that Therese was never without her little black book marked EXPENSES. Everything went into that book: every taxi fare, every souvenir, every cup of coffee she bought. I'd also noticed that when we all split a check at dinner, Therese did the arithmetic instantly in her head and remembered who had the extra feta cheese on her salad and who had the brandy afterward. Sisterhood notwithstanding, I hadn't exactly warmed up to Therese. I tend to be more casual about things like that. I prefer to put the whole check on my Visa card, figure it out later and collect what's owed me, rather than watch the waitress roll her eyes up in her head while a group of women tries to figure out how to split the tax or what kind of tip to leave. Of course, by the time I get the bill I've spent the cash I've collected, which is why I always hold my breath when they put my plastic through those little balance detectors at department stores and I don't exhale until the charge is accepted.

"Saving money is impossible," commented Margie, a thirty-two-year-old editor who'd recently broken up with her lover. "Everyone I know agrees. We've been raised on Instant Gratification—we want what we want when we want it, which is now. It's the fault of advertisers—they've created this monster. Besides, when I'm feeling low, nothing lifts me up like buying something." We all nodded. We'd scoured the shops of Athens together, buying and bargaining, and we knew that "When the going gets tough, the tough go shopping" wasn't just a slogan on Margie's T-shirt, but a way of life.

"Yes, but the guilt when you get it home . . . I cut up my credit cards at least once a year, but then I weaken, and I get new ones," said Jeanette. "The last time I saved money I lost it—passbooks were paying five percent and inflation was growing in double digits. It was just a few dollars a month, anyway—not enough to really do anything with."

"The economy is so flaky," said Merilee. "I keep wondering what would happen if I lost my job. I look at bag ladies on the street and think, *That could be me in a few years. Unless I get married.*"

"I have money I inherited, just sitting in a market account," Callie put in. "I keep thinking I should use it for a down payment on a house. It makes sense taxwise. But I keep thinking, *Someday I'll get married, then we'll buy a house together.* And I have a funny feeling about that money. After all, I didn't do anything to earn it."

"I earn mine, but I don't have time to manage it, or learn how. So I let my husband handle it," said Phyllis. "Although after hearing Harriet's story, maybe that's not such a great idea."

"I can't get over the feeling that it's just not my job, you know?" asked Ann.

"You mean, like doing your own taxes?" someone asked.

"More like taking the garbage out," Ann replied. "Yeah, and like taxes, too. There are some things men are supposed to do."

"Garbage—that's a good analogy," Kit chimed in. "Somehow, I

still think that money is sort of . . . well, unclean, you know? Evil, even."

"Why do you think, when someone gets rich, they say he made a killing?" Marcia said.

"And why is it always 'he'?" someone else asked.

Etcetera, etcetera. We all let down our financial hair like nobody's business. Which, until that evening, it had been. Our money was nobody's business—not even our own, we confessed. Of the fourteen of us, only four had IRAs, Keoghs, or any other tax-sheltered retirement investments. Another three had pension benefits from employers; one woman was hanging onto a job she intensely disliked long enough to get vested in a pension plan. Some admitted that they expected to inherit money when their parents died: "A little," said one, "A lot," said another, and "Enough" said a third.

On the topic of "enough," we were all agreed; enough was twice as much as we had, or were earning, then. No matter what the actual dollars were, we all had the idea, or the fantasy, that magically doubling the amount would provide us with that elusive thing called security, or at least a modicum of peace of mind about money.

Four of us were single mothers, and five (including Harriet) were married. Only one knew exactly how much money her husband earned—"But I didn't know that about my first husband," she said, "and I got royally screwed in my divorce settlement as a result." Except for Therese, who (no surprise) was a highly competent and well-informed manager of her finances and a sophisticated investor, we were astoundingly ignorant, misinformed, and/or uninterested in the subject of money; this group of educated, relatively affluent, mostly urban professional women spanning two generations whose family attitudes were shaped as much by national events as domestic ones—the Depression, a world war, a baby boom, and finally the participation of women in great numbers in the labor force. *How could this be?* I wondered. And why?

The answers, the explanations, and rationalizations, are in the journal I kept on that trip. They are in phrases, snatches of remembered conversations jotted down then and added to since, as I began to broach the subject with other women. Women like me, and women like you. Working women, educated women, women from poor families and rich ones, every one of us revealing in one telling phrase or another that, when it comes to money, there's some of Sleeping Beauty in us all:

- I always thought money was something men dealt with.
- I never thought I'd need to know this stuff.
- Money is something I avoid thinking about as much as I can.
- I'm hopeless with money, always have been.
- I live right up to my salary and why not? I might be dead tomorrow.
- I am scared of how much money matters to me.
- One of these days I really have to learn about money.
- I grew up believing money just happened when you got older, like wrinkles and gray hair.
- My father always doled out the money; I just assumed that some day, some other man would.
- I've never thought of the money I earn as real money. Men earn real money, women earn pin money.
- I am a miser, and I hate that in myself.
- Money is like love I can give myself.
- I learned how to manipulate men by coaxing money out of my father.
- What I'd really like to be is a middle-class housewife—before Betty Friedan.
- I know I'll never be as well off as my parents, no matter how much more I earn than they did.
- My parents still give me money. I'm really ashamed of it, but it's hard not to be seduced, even when they act as if it gives them power to control my life.
- I still feel like a little girl with money, even though I make a lot of it.

- Being mature about money is when you stop calling home collect.
- When he withholds money, it's like he's withholding love.
- For me, money is all tied up with self-esteem, even though I know it shouldn't be.
- Money fills a lot of needs I wish were filled by a man instead.

We are more comfortable talking about money than we once were, though it is still not our favorite topic; we would rather discuss relationships than something so detached from human emotion. Yet it is in emotional terms that we think about money, and we use it to meet emotional needs as much as anything else, though we may not be aware of when and how we do so. For some of us, price is a synonym for meaning; we clothe money in labels, we describe our relationships by it, we create identities and define ourselves with it. For others, value has little to do with money; we know it cannot satisfy our deepest hungers, and resist, resent, or renounce its power over us. Our messages about money are mixed and complex, and the ways in which we think and feel about it are varied and diverse. They come primarily from our functioning subconscious—Small Mind—and our personal, particularly gender-based, unconscious—Big Mind.

All of us have a psychological money style, which derives from our early experiences—what it represented in our families and what it has come, today, to stand for. We ask money to make up for what we are lacking in ourselves or in other areas of our lives: love, self-esteem, power, control, security, excitement, freedom, adulthood, purpose, character, specialness, even revenge. Making, spending, and not making money are the roles we play in our dramatized conflicts about self-worth, self-aggrandizement, and self-assertion. We put off the realization of our dreams or fantasies because of money, when money isn't what's holding us back—we are. And money represents what some of us fear most—independence.

What we need to do is "learn to depend on money for what

money can do, not be enticed into some other arrangement," suggests Edward M. Hallowell and William Grace, Jr., authors of *What Are You Worth?*[1] We need to tune into our own awareness and discover what money means to us, and what we expect from it. If those expectations are unrealistic, we can begin to develop other kinds of resources that can keep their part of the bargain.

THE DIRTY LITTLE SECRET

When my friend Pepper, who studies and writes about relationships, talks about "women's dirty little secret," it's not about sex— it's about money. And the dirty little secret is that no matter how liberated we are, how successful, how financially sophisticated, we still resent the fact that we have to think about money at all. That we have to earn it, understand it, control it, tend it, increase it, and depend on it. And with money, as with sex, what we do about it and how we feel about it are often two different things. Guilt, fear, and inadequacy often attach to it; so, too, does our sense of personal authenticity, autonomy, and connectedness. We have personal standards about both money and sex; there are some things neither money nor sex would be compelling enough to force us to do, and some offers for either (or both) that few of us could refuse. We have expectations, both negative and positive, about money: that it will enhance our lives or destroy them, make us friends or lose them, endow us with power or take it away from us.

We emotionalize money because we first experienced it in a context of dependence. Until we change its context, we can't see money for what it is, what it can and cannot do. Fathers will not always be available to rescue us, and husbands may never be; by recognizing that, we may think we have finally put the dependency demons in their place. But until we look more carefully at what we think money represents, it may be that we have only moved them to a different venue.

Jenny earns fifty-two thousand dollars annually. Fifteen years ago, when she got her M.A. in education and she entered the job market as a teacher, her starting salary was sixteen thousand dollars. "I was an idealist in the seventies when realists were getting in on the ground floor financially, going into business, getting substantial raises every year, investing in the market, buying houses at eight percent interest," she said. "Going into a low-paying career was a statement: Money didn't matter to me. It was also an expectation: I'd get married, so it wouldn't have to matter. By the time I got into business, everyone was competing for jobs, and the second wave of baby boomers was crowding up from below. I had really cynical views about money and people who made it, or controlled it. Like most people my age, I distrusted authority, especially so-called financial experts. When I left teaching, I was determined to catch up. At first I bought myself everything I hadn't been able to afford before—well, some of it, anyway. In a year, I owed almost as much as I'd earned. The market looked like a good place to recoup, and get out of debt. For a while it was. I developed a money consciousness. I put my teacher retirement fund into stocks, and I devoured the financial pages. At the top of the market, in the summer of 1987, I took some profits. Thank God. Because when it crashed, I lost the rest. Money will always be smarter, stronger, and more powerful than I will—you can't win."

Caroline, who is in her early thirties, has always been money-conscious. She grew up in a poor family, and opened her first bank account when she was twelve, with money she earned babysitting. She put herself through college, and spending money, she says, "has always been like pulling my own teeth." But only on herself; with her friends, lover, and younger sisters and brothers, she is extremely generous. She went into banking because, to her, bankers had power. "They took my family's farm away," she said. "I wasn't ever going to let them take anything of mine." In fact, she now realizes, her family lost the farm not because tornadoes destroyed the crops—they didn't—or wheat prices fell—they rose—but because her father compensated for a life he hated on a farm he inherited by giving or gambling away all its profits, and eventually all his money. Once, Caroline remembers, he took all the cash from one season's crop and bought his two teenage daughters shiny new convertibles. Her mother remade old clothes, recooked leftovers, and scrimped and saved wherever she could to compensate, a behavior pattern Caroline has repeated, just as she repeats her father's profligate generosity.

When Trina's parents died, she inherited a hundred thousand dollars. "Until then, my friends and I were in pretty similar circumstances, financially speaking," she said. "Nobody was poor, but no one was rich, either. And all of a sudden, I was. I hadn't done anything to deserve it, and I felt guilty. Or separate. Or something. So I gave it away." She didn't really gave it away—she lent it to others. "I helped one friend start a restaurant. I financed another's car. I subsidized someone who was trying to finish a novel she was sure would enable her to pay me back. I thought of it as 'alternative banking.' I charged them the same amount of interest I would have received on a passbook account—somehow, that made it OK. I wasn't profiting from the loans, but I wasn't losing money, either. And I learned how money can really mess up, or even just change, relationships between people. I found myself making judgments about my friends based on how they did or didn't repay me, how they spent their own money, whether they were extravagant or cheap. I thought it was money that was getting in the way; really, it was guilt that I couldn't acknowledge."

Some women displace all their other worries onto money. Often it isn't money that's at the bottom of things at all, but feelings of emotional insecurity, lack of self-esteem, loss of love, fear of the future. It's hard to think about these things; money offers a convenient repository for unmanageable anxieties or conflicts.

Other women go to enormous lengths to avoid thinking about money at all. They say it bores them with its picky details, but what they feel is anxious about the decision-making that money entails. Occasionally they make attempts to get it organized, under control, in the right place, but often they give up after a few tries. These are women who earn it and ignore it; money success makes them nervous or guilty, so money slips right through their fingers, and then they don't have to think about it.

There's hardly a woman alive who hasn't, at one time or another, used money as an antidepressant. But for the truly depressed, it doesn't help for long. It doesn't address the real issue of depression, which is the absence of emotional energy that's necessary to cope with the problems depression may be masking—some of which can be helped by medication, others by therapy. The flip side of treating depression with money is that guilt often follows—it's like breaking a diet with candy.

Some women are manic by nature and money is the way they express emotional mood swings. Money feeds their grandiose and unrealistic dreams, allows them to flee the painful feelings that are at the heart of those moods. "When I was depressed about a work situation that wouldn't clear up, I bought a grand piano I couldn't afford—I don't even know how to play," said Kate. When my own mother died and I inherited money, I spent it manically for a thankfully brief time. When I was able, finally, to grieve in a less destructive way, my urge to spend disappeared.

Overspending is more often a woman's problem than a man's, although we all do it sometimes. "We think of money as a useful tool in short supply," says Dr. Hallowell. "Our agreement is, If I spend it, it will make me feel better, and often that works." But this money style becomes disabling when either the real debt becomes too great or the ability to cope becomes too small. Suddenly you feel you have no control over your financial life and you panic—not just about money, but about all aspects of your life, even those that are under control. And you've become a worrier, displacing your other fears onto money.

Overspending is circular illogic. By doing it we create that feeling of not having enough which is what we think we're curing by doing it in the first place. When we mix up our emotions with our money, which most of us do at one time or another, we're assigning money parts it can't play in our own personal psychodramas, because external gains cannot compensate for internal lacks or losses. When we see it as a tool to make our lives easier, buy us the things only money can buy, and don't let it compromise the parts of our life that are equally if not more important—creativity, love, autonomy—we are on our way to coming to terms with it at last.

Establishing a congruent relationship between money and personal values is extremely important to women, particularly those who feel that, in one way or another, they have "sold out" in order to acquire money, by working at a job they hate, by trading the economic security of a marriage or other relationship for the uncertainty of making it on one's own, by accepting unearned money in the form of an inheritance or some other stroke of luck. The newspapers are full of stories about lottery winners who blow it all on extravagant purchases, as if they couldn't wait to get rid of it. Money can stand between you as you are and you as you'd like to be, unless you are capable, with money or without, of acting in a way that matches your personal value system and thus permits you to use what you have to make your life, or the lives of others, more comfortable. Money can be dangerous when it is a factor in a relationship, especially if it is the woman who has more. Whether it is a woman and her husband, or a mother and her child, a woman wielding the purse strings is a woman responding to culturally imbued cues about power and control; and the possibility that she might misuse it and so alter or destroy her relationships is a frightening one.

Knowing what your conscious and unconscious agreements with money are about can be liberating as well as painful. Understanding how you express certain aspects of your personality with money—your generosity or fearfulness, your optimism or pessimism, your self-image as autonomous or other-directed—can provide you with insights about what you believe money can do. But along with psychological insights must come some baseline data about where you are right now, financially speaking, so that you can begin to establish goals for where you want to be—next month, next year, or even longer than that. Yes, a life partner may enter the picture at some time. So might a child. If that happens, you'll want to rethink those goals and establish other ones. But the real bottom line is that then, as now, you will need enough money to take care of your own needs. And before you can conceptualize "enough," you need to know where you currently stand. So your money history will have dollar signs as well as psychological insights, actual amounts as well as symbolic representations. From your own net-worth statement, you can begin to create a model that will guide you in managing your finances rationally, and in a way that fits your style, psychology, and conscious and unconscious agreements about money.

Too many of us base our spending and investing decisions on what the experts have told us is right, instead of what we know about ourselves. My favorite analogy about budgets, balance sheets, and investment plans is a diet; I always do better on a diet that features foods I like rather than those I hate. The smartest money plan in the world won't work if I won't stick to it, because, even though it's healthful, I hate the taste.

THE SINGLE WOMAN'S LUXURY BUDGET
The lives of married friends lose some of their charm when you consider all the demands on their money, from orthodontia for the children to bigger houses to accommodate their growing families. Single women, by contrast, have much more disposable income; there are fewer liens on our futures, more slack in the here and now. College annuities are what couples buy with left-over cash; comfort, pleasure, and luxury are the payoffs for a single woman's budget. Carla keeps a credit card just for those kinds of items. She never charges anything that could be even remotely described as a necessity—"flowers, plane tickets, clothes I could never wear to the office, impulse-buying kinds of things. Nothing that's already accounted for in my planning. Things that meet needs I'm not even consciously aware of. My card has a five-hundred dollar limit, and has to be paid off in full every

month, which also means there's no service charge. Some months I spend right up to my limit. Other times I don't, so I put an equal amount into an account for big-ticket luxuries, like vacations, a new car, a fur coat. It's a matter of putting a price on my self-indulgence, which makes me feel I can handle it, it's never out of control. I used to be a chronic overspender—at the end of the month, I'd wonder where it all went. Now I know."

Ruth takes a hundred dollars in ten-dollar bills out of every paycheck and spends her lunch hour on the first floor of a department store. "I never go above that floor, because that's where the expensive things are," she says. "I come home with scarves, cosmetics, notions, a belt, gloves, stuff like that. I only spend cash. Using credit cards is fooling yourself—you think you haven't spent anything, that putting down the card is the same as paying for it. Spending actual cash is thrilling, exciting—spending plastic is self-deluding."

"All the books say, 'Pay yourself first,'" Megan says. "I do. For every dollar I put in savings or investments, I put ten cents in my mad-money account. It's for a different kind of security: the security of knowing I can splurge on frivolous things or luxuries without mortgaging my old age. I used to be a real miser with money—spending it on anything that wasn't absolutely necessary was very hard for me. I don't expect to marry; I don't really want to. But I have this specter looming over me of being a poor old lady, shivering in the cold because there's no money to pay the electric bill. I didn't touch my luxury account for two years after I started it. The first thing I bought with it was a fur coat. At least I won't be cold when I'm old."

Dory, who earns a good salary as an advertising copywriter, takes on extra free-lance assignments to satisfy her craving for expensive clothes. She makes a wardrobe budget every season, spends what's allocated, and takes on as much work as she needs to buy the extras or more expensive, unbudgeted items. "I look at a job as a designer suit, or a pair of Italian leather boots," she says. "I'd rather earn more than spend less. And in some ways I enjoy doing those assignments more than I enjoy my regular work. I only put my extra money somewhere I can emotionally move it."

"I have always avoided using money in ways that would make my life more comfortable, more luxurious," says Susan. "I always blamed whatever was wrong with my life on money, or the lack of it. When I'm more willing to face the reasons for my unhappiness—which have nothing to do with money—I feel freer to spend it. I couldn't bring myself to buy a house until I got over grieving for a relationship that ended badly. I felt like I didn't deserve to have it. When I told my parents I was going to buy a condo, they said it was dumb. My mother said, 'What does a single woman need with her own house?' My father said, 'You'll find a guy, then you'll get a place together.' It wasn't until I pointed out the tax advantages you get with a house that they stopped nagging me about it."

In fact, it is those high-ticket items—houses, jewelry, even furs—that many women avoid purchasing, even when they have ample funds available. Somehow, those are the things that men are supposed to buy for us, and the Sleeping Beauty in us prefers to wait. And wait. And wait. We leave excess funds in passbook savings, the financial equivalent of burying money in the back yard, because a stock portfolio, like a mortgage, seems somehow inappropriate for a single woman. We indulge ourselves in the freedom to spend rather than shouldering the responsibility to save or invest. We live in a dreamlike trance, emotionally trapped between the (mythical) protection of two men, the father king and the lover Prince. The implied message of the fairy tale we live by is, as Bruno Bettleheim says: "Don't worry, don't try to make something happen; when the time is right, the wall of thorns will disappear, the Prince will enter, and the impossible problem [in this case, money] will be solved, effortlessly, as if by itself."[2]

ANGIE—TAKING A FLYER ON LOVE
The only reason I ever look forward to going to the dentist is Angie. She's been taking care of my teeth for ten years, and she

never uses words like "a little discomfort"; when it's going to hurt, she tells you, and that in itself makes it less painful than it otherwise might be.

When I met Angie, she'd been divorced for several years. Childless and independent, she enjoyed an enviable life-style. She dated regularly, but until she met Glen she'd never considered remarrying. She didn't need a husband, but she wanted one; when she fell in love with Glen, she thought she'd found him.

"What attracted me was his independence," Angie said. "He seemed very free. He wasn't tied to a career or profession, a uniform, or a three-piece suit. He'd get a temporary job when he needed money, and when he had enough to quit, he'd quit for a while, to work on the boat he'd been building for several years. He lived simply, but with a certain bohemian style I found very appealing. He didn't care about money. If he couldn't afford something, he did without it. When I was with him, jug wine tasted like champagne and daisies smelled like roses. He was very carefree and devil-may-care, and maybe because I always had a really bourgeois attitude about money—that's why I went into dentistry, if you want to know the truth—his insouciance was very appealing. And his life-style seemed romantic; he had fantasies about finishing the boat and casting off and sailing around the world, picking up work and money when he needed to. I bought right into his fantasy—remember, I'd gone from college to graduate school and into my own practice and teaching, and in sixteen years of doing that a lot of my own escape fantasies just sort of faded away.

"When we began living together, money wasn't an issue. He bought groceries, and he remodeled my kitchen. I paid for a couple of vacations we took. We worked on the boat together on weekends. So when we decided to get married, I didn't think anything would change. Other people did—my friends and my parents. My best friend actually said, 'Angie, are you buying yourself a husband?' It was that crass.

"And the answer I came up with—not to her, but to myself—

was, *What if I am?* I had money—what better place to put it than in a future with a man I loved? And Glen was giving up his independence—he made it seem like that was a fair trade."

If it was, Angie said ruefully, "it was no bargain. Glen quit his job in order to finish the boat in time for my sabbatical. When my partner and I opened our office, we agreed we would each take one year off, in turn, after our financial goals were met. She used her year off to have a baby; I was going to use mine to live out this incredibly romantic fantasy and sail around the world with the man I loved."

After a few months, Glen decided it would be more efficient to hire and supervise a crew to complete the boat in time for Angie's planned sabbatical. "He was lousy as a supervisor," she said. "He'd tell the guys to knock off early and they'd all go out for a beer. Or they wouldn't show up at all, and he wouldn't fire them. He was even worse as a businessman—he'd vastly underestimate equipment costs, labor, everything, so that it all cost twice as much as we thought it would. He kept enlarging the plans—now that it was for the two of us, he said, he had to make it bigger, safer, more comfortable. Of course, when my sabbatical started, the boat wasn't finished. And I was in so much deeper financially that I was going to have to cut it in half and only take six months, anyway."

By the time the boat was done, a year and a half later, Angie and Glen were divorced. "He wasn't a househusband, and he wasn't a housewife, either. Not only didn't he shop, cook, or clean—he didn't do anything. He had no energy to put into the relationship, the house, the project. I was putting everything in, and getting nothing back, not even sex or love—just this deadness. He wasn't like the man I'd fallen in love with—he'd fallen apart. He was incredibly dependent, which I couldn't stand—I, who never even wanted children. He accused me of using money to make up for what I wasn't giving—what he said husbands were entitled to: emotional support. And he was right. I was paying the bills; I wanted him to give *me* those things."

Angie never wanted money to be a symbol of power in her marriage. "But it was—it can't help but be," she said. "I still believe that investing money as well as love in a relationship can work, even though in this case it didn't. I think if we had dealt with it up front—really talked about what my having money and his not having it meant in terms of our expectations, our ambitions, and our reversing traditional roles—we could have gotten past it. Both of us thought more about using money than how it was using, and abusing, us. Money, in the end, was a substitute for intimacy, for the kind of meshing of values and meaning you need in a real relationship."

Having money may make some women as vulnerable as not having it makes other women. Dena, a successful interior designer, was swept off her feet and into a three-star love affair with a man she met on a business trip to California. He flew to Atlanta twice a month to see her, and in between there were romantic weekends, flowers by wire, and plans for the future. On the basis of those plans, she "lent" him fifty thousand dollars. It wasn't until a private detective hired by another woman to check into her "fiancé's" background caught up with Dena that she learned Matt had swindled many other women out of money, too. "Based only on the ones he told me about, the totals were in the neighborhood of two million dollars," Dena told me. "I testified at his trial on wire-fraud charges, as did three of his other victims. All of us were otherwise intelligent women—not millionaires, but with substantial businesses or practices, comfortable life-styles, and status in our professions and communities. We were all attractive women, confident, and self-assured. None of us ever dreamed a man would want us for our money—that's the kind of thing that happens to heiresses."

Not these days. Women who command high salaries, who have investments and property and other assets, are increasingly suspicious of men who seem more interested in their bottom lines than their bottoms themselves, as Dena put it. "There's no doubt that having money increases a woman's attractiveness, just as it does a man's," says Gena, a successful realtor. "Yet it isn't something we want to admit, even to ourselves. My boyfriend isn't bothered by the fact that I have more money than he does, but I am. Sometimes I wonder whether, if I didn't have it, he'd still want me. And then I think, *Well, I do, so why torture myself with meaningless questions like that?* In that way, having money makes me less secure, not more secure. I'll be glad when he finishes his residency and finally starts earning money. I don't want to get married until then, I just have this thing about wanting a man to be more powerful than I am—or at least, as powerful—and I guess that means money. I'm not proud of those feelings, but I still have them."

A NEST EGG FOR NOW, ANOTHER FOR LATER

It's very easy to use money as an excuse not to do what we say we want to do. I once wanted to trek around South America like my friends Dace and Carol. They were roommates in law school, who promised themselves they'd do that together some day. I met them a year before they left, and I followed them from Guatemala to Tierra del Fuego via postcards, letters, and an occasional phone call. Whenever my life seemed particularly gray and dreary, I imagined them on a beach in the Galapagos Islands, or in a conga line in Rio. If I'd had enough money, I could have gone, too.

A few years later, I helped Sally move into a country cabin, after she'd quit her job to write a novel. She'd worked for ten years to buy herself a year and as I drove down the mountain road away from her bucolic retreat, I thought, *I'd do that, too, if I had the money*

For the last couple of years I've eaten cheap Mexican food with Bea instead of splurging at the food mafia's latest discovery because Bea was going back to school for her master's degree after she'd saved enough money. And I've gone on a couple of trips without Peggy, because she was saving her money for a six-month leave without pay to go to a Buddhist retreat in the desert. Every time I watch someone make a dream happen by dint of delaying gratification and saving for what they really want, I judge myself, and find me wanting. I do save, but it's for the future—the far future. And I keep a liquid stash for emergencies. It's the "meantime" I have trouble with—that chunk of vital life between now and old age when it's time to put my other dreams to the test. If I really dared to try them, I'd have a nest egg for sooner as well as for later.

When I stop to think of all the things I thought I'd do if I had the money, I realize that the ones I truly did want to do, I did. I didn't think I could afford a house until I saw one that whispered seductively, *I'm yours.* And then in three months I worked harder than I ever had, taking extra assignments, cutting out all but the necessities, and scraped together enough for a down payment. I didn't think I could afford to move across the country, find work and friends and a place to live, but I did that too, and made it happen, with some careful planning, bartering, switching of apartments, and such. I didn't think I could afford to quit my job until it made me so crazy I couldn't afford not to.

PUTTING YOUR MONEY WHERE YOUR MOUTH IS

We do the things we really want to do, and the others we rationalize away by saying we can't afford it. The nest egg for now is a way of testing our mid-life desires against the fantasies we had a while back. If we still want them or dare to go for them, we will always find a way to afford them. Fantasies fade when not fed or nurtured at all. When they truly become goals, you'll maximize the assets you have now—money and energy—and find a way to accomplish them. Money is synonymous with freedom in that it makes possible experiences you might otherwise not have. But, as Michael Phillips says in *The Seven Laws of Money:*

> In most cases, no change in the availability of money is going to change a person's priorities. People usually know what they want to do, but they're unwilling to acknowledge whatever it is within their personality that makes them do

what they're doing and leads to their self-deception. People invariably have scapegoats, and money has always been one of the most convenient ones, because it is commonly agreed that we can't do most of the things we want to do because we don't have enough money."[3]

THE PERILS OF FINANCIAL ILLITERACY

This isn't the place for a dollars-and-cents discussion of how to plan, spend, and save your money. There are dozens of good books, qualified experts, and other sources of wisdom to help you decide on a financial strategy that fits your emotional as well as economic needs. Nearly every one of those books has a sample balance sheet, net-worth statement, profit-and-loss chart. They all tell you the secret to financial success is to plan for future as well as present needs, diversify your holdings, pay attention to which way the economy is heading, and expect everything to get more expensive in the years to come. All I can add to that is this: Learning to manage your money and making it work with you instead of against you can be a terrific high. You can do it. You *must* do it. Yes, there are risks involved. But all you are risking is money—not love, self-esteem, freedom, or meaning. There are always ways to get more money, but if you give money power over more important things, it won't be worth what it cost. Money cannot transform or protect you; only you can do that.

The price of financial illiteracy is a high one. While there are worlds without money—the worlds of art, sex, love, poetry, the mind, the body, and the spirit—we live in one where money is exchanged for the means to sustain those. As Michael Phillips says, "There is somewhere without money. You can't reach it except by focusing on the non-money parts of your life—what you do, how you work, who you are, and who you associate with. But we are in the money, just as a fish is in the water, and recognition of this can greatly influence how we respond to the world around us."[4]

Money cannot buy imagination, passion, or creativity, but it

can be the cornerstone of emotional as well as financial freedom—
if we let it be. No matter how solvent we are, or how successful,
the real turning point in our relationship with money will be
reached when we face the fact that we may not marry. At that
point, Sleeping Beauties can begin to look realistically at where
they are now, decide where they want to be later, and understand
that money is a tool when it's saved or invested, not just when it's
spent. If life circumstances change and we enter into a relationship, the personal values and goals we establish right now about
money will stand us in good stead. The hard facts are that women
earn less money than men do, and live longer. Beauty may be
willing to risk everything for love, but when it's her long-term
financial security at stake, she may be making a very expensive
gamble.

❋ 8 ❋

Catch 35: Do You Really Want a Child?

Once upon a time, most of us—Sleeping Beauties as well as self-defined women—expected that someday we would find the Prince, and together we'd produce the ideal family. These days, those who are still unmarried are somewhat cynical about the Prince, but we haven't given up on that ideal family. And some Beauties who've forsaken the couch for the world beyond the castle still hold that ideal image close to their hearts. Not only that; they're going ahead with their plans, regardless of whether or not there's a Prince, or even a frog, in the picture. It's just that their ideal family looks a little different these days. But is it really?

Now that my nest is emptying, many of my friends are furnishing theirs. They waited to have children until they'd done everything else; I waited to do everything else until after I'd had children. I never planned to be a single mother, but that was the way it turned out, and while it wasn't always a day at the beach, it wasn't as bad as I thought it would be. Or maybe I just don't remember. After all, they're grown and gone now. It's been years since I sat up in bed in the middle of the night, wondering who would take care of them if something happened to me, hoping that in the morning they wouldn't ask the strange man at the breakfast table if he was going to be their daddy; worrying that if the transmission didn't last a few more weeks they couldn't go to summer camp.

Being their sole support, the only consistent presence in their lives, their flimsy protection against a sometimes unpredictable and always uncontrollable world, was a responsibility I was glad to put down when the time came—as I never, in those days, thought it would. In the interim, I fantasized about an Other who would save me—who would save us all. He never did, so we had to save each other, but that might not have taken as long as it did if I'd planned it that way from the start.

If I'd expected to be a single mother, I'd have done things differently. I'd have learned to ask for help without feeling that I'd failed—that if I'd been smarter or stronger or wiser I wouldn't need help in the first place. I'd have established my career, arrived at a place where I felt vocationally secure, one that included flexible working conditions and summers and holidays off. I'd have paid all my debts, saved some money (even though it never would have been enough), and arranged for a line of credit with no (emotional) strings attached. I'd have made all those friends I never thought I needed when I was married, and didn't begin to appreciate until I was divorced. I'd have taken more vacations on islands with no telephones, knowing that it would be eighteen years before I could do it again.

So when the friends who now wake up in the middle of the night worrying that they'll never have the worries that woke me up in the middle of the night ask me if I'd do it again, I don't know what to tell them. Because I never made a choice to do it the way they're planning to do it—alone. And maybe that's what makes all the difference.

They are caught in the Catch 35 of their generation. It may not be too late to marry, but it is almost too late to have a child. Some are professionally successful by volition, single and childless by default. They didn't "decide" to concentrate on careers rather than families, although that's a prevailing popular assumption; it just worked out that way. For a few—even those who greatly desire children—it isn't a crisis. They immerse themselves in work, friends, travel, and hobbies, form intimate and durable relationships that provide a sense of community and continuity—often with other people's children.

For other women, however, Catch 35—or 30 or 40 or more—*is* a crisis. They may not be ready to be wives, but they *are* ready to be mothers, and more of them are going ahead anyway, whether or not they're involved in a close, committed, intimate relationship. Most would happily settle down if they found the right man, but they've been fooled by love before and won't marry just to have a child. Some who have always preferred to be single are no longer feeling that they need to be married to make having a child OK. And others who cannot justify their decisions on rational grounds are leaving it to their bodies to decide.

Intentional single motherhood is one of a wide range of options that independent, autonomous women are considering today. Enough of them have elected it to represent a statistically significant number. The birthrate in the last decade for unmarried white women between thirty and thirty-four has increased 59 percent; for thirty-five to thirty-nine-year-olds, the rate rose by 45 percent.[1] Since most adult women know how to prevent or terminate a pregnancy, it's a safe assumption that choice played a major role in these births. The phenomenon of single motherhood is not a new one; what is new is its increasing prevalence among middle-class women, many, but not all of whom are approaching the limits of their fertility.

For the majority of the one hundred socially mainstream, educated professional women over twenty-five who responded to Sharyne Merrit and Linda Steiner's 1984 survey of unmarried mothers,[2] timing was a key factor in their decision, related more to concerns about their age and/or fertility than to whether they had achieved other personal, professional, or financial goals. A few of these women elected to become single mothers before their thirtieth birthdays. Some in both groups chose adoption rather than conception. They did so because they had difficulty achieving or maintaining pregnancy; could not find or did not want either natural or donor fathers for their children; or because adoption still enjoys wider acceptance as a socially sanctioned option for women who want children without husbands than unmarried conception. As far back as the beginning of the century, independent single women were adopting children on their own; they were admired for their unselfishness and praised for their generosity in giving good homes to poor orphans. Unmarried pregnant women (or girls) who raised their own children were considered pariahs. Times are more tolerant today. But even now, in some regions of the country, in some professions and institutions, and in some segments of the population, an unmarried woman bearing a natural child is subject to scorn, gossip, or condemnation. "I knew getting pregnant would finish my career," said Rachel, an elementary school principal from a small town in the South. "I might have the law on my side—legally, they can't fire me, although they certainly don't have to promote me, either. But when I adopted my daughter from an orphanage in India— well, they treated me like I was Mother Teresa."

Would-be single mothers are often confronting that attitude even among medical professionals. *"Especially* in the profession," comments Dr. Richard Soderstrom, a fertility specialist who has been a longtime proponent of a woman's right to choose. I met him when we worked together on a committee to liberalize abortion laws in Washington, and when I saw him again seventeen years later, he had just returned from marching on the nation's capital on behalf of *Roe* vs. *Wade.* Even he admits that he has to overcome his own misgivings when a single woman asks his assistance in bearing a child. "I have memories of the old days when I was an attending physician at the Florence Crittenden home for unwed mothers," he says. "I know how many of the women who kept their babies then regretted their decisions—how often those babies ended up abused, in trouble, or fostered out. Although I don't suppose you're talking about those kinds of women. The women you mean are adults; they're capable, self-reliant, and prepared for single motherhood. Unfortunately, not all of my colleagues see the distinction."

Word gets around, however. Women who want children seek out and find physicians to help them make their dreams come true, who have compassion for a single woman's yearning to be a mother through natural conception or artificial insemination. And that's the easy way; when it comes to adoption, most single women will have a harder time than their married friends in finding a healthy infant to adopt in this country. Agencies, doctors, and lawyers reserve the few they know about for couples. "It may not be fair, but who said life was fair?" Dr. Soderstrom asks. "If that's what you want—if that's your fantasy child—you'll probably have to find a man who's willing to help you."

In the more urban environments, it doesn't seem to matter whether a woman has a child by conceiving or adopting; single motherhood has become chic and even fashionable. Movie stars do it, without the opprobrium that Ingrid Bergman suffered once upon a time, and so do less visible but equally determined women. "Oh, Mother," said one of them to her own mother, who was pleasantly surprised when the friends to whom she'd nervously confided the news of her banker daughter's pregnancy thought it was a courageous and praiseworthy event, "only in New York do you get points for having a divorced, pregnant, unwed daughter!"[3]

Being on top of a trend isn't much of a reason to have a child whether you're single or married. But feelings of exclusion or alienation from friends who are doing just that prompts many single women to consider motherhood on their own terms. So may a change in a woman's circumstances: a relationship ends, a parent dies, a particular rung on the career ladder is achieved, a financial goal is accomplished, a landmark birthday is reached. A life that was rich and full seems somehow lacking in an essential element. The future becomes as important as the present—maybe even more so. There is a sense that it is time to move into a new phase of life.

A woman knows it in her body, mind, and feelings. Something stirs in the deepest, most hidden levels of her awareness, and when she pays attention—when she brings her intelligence, intuitiveness, and insight to bear on her emotions—she confronts what will be the most important decision of her life. Regardless of what that decision is, the process of making it—of conscious, active choosing—inexorably changes her.

LAURA—"I HAVE A LOT TO OFFER A CHILD"

We came out blinking, the way you do when you've been in a theater in the middle of the day and realize that outside it's still daylight. We dodged limos and taxis and buses, the traffic of a matinee Wednesday in Manhattan's theater district, and walked back to the Plaza where we sprawled out on the twin beds in Laura's room and caught up on each other's lives. We live in the same city, a continent away, but we both had business in New York that week and we'd both wanted to see *The Heidi Chronicles*, Wendy Wasserstein's Pulitzer Prize–winning drama about a unique but not uncommon woman—a smart, successful, single woman. She's scared, the way many women are these days, women who always expected to have a child but still haven't. Scared the way Laura, a thirty-nine-year-old pediatrician, is scared.

Just how scared I didn't realize until Laura told me she was going to have a baby, too. Just like Heidi, the heroine of the play, who, as the final curtain descends, adopts a child, Laura was going to do it—not with a husband, or even a lover, but all by herself. "Well, not entirely by myself," she said. "I'm expecting my friends to help . . . won't you?"

"Well, sure," I gulped. But had she thought all this through?

Being Laura—determined, independent, highly motivated, and self-directed Laura—she had. She had the how and the why figured out, she said—she just wasn't sure of the who yet.

The why was easy. Laura has always wanted a child. She had an abortion fifteen years ago, while she was in medical school, and although time has dimmed the memory, it is still painful and, lately, very present. As a pediatrician, she is in contact with infants and children every day and yearns for her own. By anyone's standards, Laura's life is full, rich, and rewarding. What's missing from it is not a husband; although she's had several serious relationships, she has been content to be single, and believes she will continue to feel that way. She's done everything she ever wanted or needed to do: "I've hitchhiked through Europe, I lived in a commune, I've had plenty of adventures. I've given myself what I wanted; now I want to give to someone else. Not just things, and not just love, but myself. I have a lot to offer a child. In the last few years, I've had a very strong feeling that it's time to change my life. At first I thought it was my career, remember?"

I nodded. After a decade on staff at an HMO, Laura dropped out. She signed on as a cruise ship doctor, and did that for a while, and then she worked weekend shifts in the emergency room, spending the other five days throwing pots, buying a new house, remodeling it, and planting a garden. Then she joined a group practice with three other women physicians. She told me then that her "time out" had made her a little older, a little wiser; she knew that pediatrics was what she wanted to do, and she took a residency in that specialty. Her current professional situation is a good one—rewarding, secure, relatively flexible, and potentially lucrative.

"I realized, finally, that I don't need to be married, but I *do* want to be connected and committed to someone—to a child, not a husband. It's a different kind of fulfillment I'm looking for," she said. Unlike Heidi, Laura does not want to adopt. "I know it sounds conceited and selfish, but I've got good genes and a good heritage. I want to pass them on to my own child."

THE SPERM BANK VERSUS LOVE WITH THE PROPER STRANGER

Since there's no Significant Other in Laura's life right now, she's been looking into artificial insemination. She's researched sperm banks all over the country, including the Repository for Germinal Choice, which is the so-called Nobel sperm bank (although, since not that many prize winners were willing to seed the next generation of geniuses, the RGC makes do with the sperm of lesser mortals, who are all carefully selected for optimal genetic contributions). She also found banks that will ship frozen sperm on demand to prospective mothers or their physicians. But then she ruled out AI. "I can't see myself answering a child's questions about 'where did I come from'—not when the answer is a test tube. I'd like to know something about the biological coparent, at least be able to describe him to a child. No ... it'll either be someone I know, or the proverbial stranger in the night."

Where, in these sexually dangerous times, does a woman find a stranger—a safe stranger? Laura suggested that a good place to look might be at the medical conference that was her reason for being in New York that week. "A majority of sperm donors are physicians or medical students anyway, but frankly, I'd prefer one who wants to make a more personal kind of deposit," she said with a grin. "I'm making a fairly reasonable assumption that a conscientious man who's also a doctor wouldn't have sex with me if he had any reason to believe he'd been exposed to a sexually transmitted disease."

While doctors and hospitals have traditionally used financially strapped and presumably healthy medical students as donors, the concept of sperm banks is relatively recent. Many physicians still feel that fresh sperm is more reliable than the frozen variety (although there is relatively little data to support this theory). However, with the advent of AIDS, frozen sperm is the only available choice for banks operating under the protocols of the American College of Fertility; before it is inseminated into a woman, sperm must be tested and retested, not just for AIDS but for a number of other diseases and conditions. "If a woman has a partner, or even a good friend, by whom she can be artificially inseminated—because she does not wish to have intercourse, because he is impotent, or for any other reason—we test the donor, and then use fresh sperm," says Dr. Soderstrom. "In my own experience, the results are generally better and more reliable than they are with frozen semen. But that's not always an option."

Most women who choose artificial insemination do so because they do not want the actual or potential legal or emotional complications that may ensue when a natural biological father is involved. Women desiring to have a child by a natural father should look carefully into present laws regarding the rights and responsibilities of fathers, acknowledged or not. The laws are changing— not fast enough to keep up with social change, perhaps, but too fast for women who assume that if they bear the child alone, its natural father has neither rights nor responsibilities. The anonymity of most bank-supplied donors is guaranteed, and as yet, no presumptive father whose sperm was supplied through a bank has come forth to claim, or disclaim, a child.

Laura does not want to have a child *with* any of the men she knows; having one *by* one of them is a different matter. But thus far she hasn't had much luck. The only man she's broached the subject with who hasn't turned her down flat is an ex-lover, and he wants to be more deeply involved in raising a child than she wants him to be. She next asked a married man—over the years, they've had an intermittent sexual relationship, although she says now that the affair is coming to an end. "He was worried about what might happen if someday the child turns up and says, 'Hi, Pop.' What would his wife and their kids say?" Laura reported. She also asked Steve, a close, platonic friend who is single and has expressed his fear that he'll never find someone he wants to share his life with. He didn't believe that Laura would make no other requests except his sperm; like many men, he was suspicious that she wanted more.

Laura's failure to strike a bargain with someone she knows is typical of the experience of many women who make similar requests of friends or lovers. It's not surprising; when a woman says, "This is going to be *my* child, conceived out of *my* body, out of *my* desire," few men are willing to consciously cooperate, even if it means they'll be unacknowledged or uninvolved. "They may not want the responsibility of a child, but they don't *not* want it either—at least not that way," says Laura. Many men drift away from their children once the relationship with their mother is over, regardless of whether or not they were married to her, as statistics on divorced fathers who provide no financial support for their children indicate. But Laura knew that her ex-lover wouldn't do that, which was why she decided against him. "If he's in my child's life—and believe me, he *would* be—he'll be in mine. And I don't want that, which is why we broke up. He would have been a terrible husband, and he'd be a worse father. So no. But after all those turn-downs, I have to tell you, I was tempted. He wanted to get married, and I only want marriage to the right man on the right terms. When I told him I wasn't ready to be a wife, only a mother, he said, 'If you can't make a success of a relationship, you've naive to think you can succeed as a mother, either.'"

IF YOU'RE NOT READY FOR MARRIAGE, ARE YOU READY FOR MOTHERHOOD?

Having a baby with a husband or partner doesn't insure that you'll raise it with him—not when one out of two marriages ends in divorce, not at a time when 41 percent of children under eighteen live in single-parent households headed by women. And forging a successful man/woman relationship doesn't require the same skills as raising a child. In a marriage, the key issues are power, sex, compatibility, sharing, and mutual goals; as a parent, other qualities and traits, such as the capacity to nurture and protect, the strength for continuous, one-way giving, and the willingness to offer unqualified love and acceptance to a child are necessary. Laura frankly admits she's not ready for marriage, and may never be. But she is very certain that she is ready for motherhood.

She says her desire, and her decision, are supported by her friends, colleagues, social network, and family. "When I told my mother what I was thinking about doing, she said, 'Oh, *could* we?' She is totally in favor, completely supportive. She never expected me to get married, anyway—she always said I wouldn't find any-one who'd measure up to my standards, and maybe she's right."

Intentional single mothers are often characterized as selfish, self-indulgent, or morally confused. The degree to which a woman responds to or is hurt by these attitudes depends on how much she internalizes society's, or someone else's, judgment. The opinions of people who do not share Laura's attitude are not as important to her as they are to some women. "You really are serious about this, aren't you?" I asked. "Serious, yes," Laura replied. "Absolutely certain? Not quite, but I'm getting there."

CHOOSING NOT TO CHOOSE

Like many of the women who come to the "thinker" groups offered by Single Mothers by Choice, a national organization formed four years ago by Jane Mattes, a psychotherapist and the mother of an eight-year-old son, Laura has still not made a firm decision, although she says she is getting closer to it all the time. Only a small percentage of the women who come to these groups actually follow through with single motherhood, according to Dr. Mattes. They may not yet feel emotionally or financially secure enough, or they may sense or know that their motivations are not psychologically healthy or valid. The best reason for choosing single motherhood is the desire to enhance, not compensate for, the quality of one's life. But for some women, the desire to parent is based on other needs; some are neurotic and some are normal. The woman who wants a child for its own sake, and hopes the rewards will outweigh the difficulties, is normal; the woman who wants it just to show the world she can do it alone better than others who do it together is less so.

What every woman who has even considered bearing or adopting a child on her own knows is that such a decision is not to be taken lightly; it is a commitment you cannot walk away from. Wanting a commitment of that magnitude is a benchmark of maturity; as Dr. William Menninger said, one of the "symptoms" of adulthood is the readiness to accept responsibility joyfully and willingly.

The motivation and attitude of a single mother counts more than anything else in determining the quality of her relationship with her child and her happiness in life. If, like Laura, you feel that your basic emotional needs are already met—if you feel valued, affirmed, and acknowledged, good about yourself and satisfied with your life, secure that your decision is socially and morally acceptable to those who matter, fulfilled in your work and confident about your ability to parent alone—then single motherhood may be one of the options that is open to you as an independent, autonomous, and self-actualizing woman. If not, it isn't an option, but a mistake that may have disastrous consequences for everyone involved.

WHAT ARE THE ODDS ON HAPPINESS?

In every respect, Laura fits the profile, if such exists, of the woman most likely to succeed as a single mother by choice. She is highly motivated, determined, and independent by nature. She is also self-directed and committed, traits that will be necessary if her efforts to find a natural father are unsuccessful and she resorts to AI, which can be an expensive and time-consuming business. She is financially and professionally secure, she has a full life and wants to share it. The moment of choice, she feels, is upon her.

"I always held out the hope that the right guy would come along, but I can't wait anymore. I'm already in the high-risk category," she said. She reeled off the statistics: At her age, the odds of bearing a Down's syndrome child jump from one in 1500, typical of women under thirty, to one in 280. Fertility, too, falls off dramatically; only 53.6 percent of women over thirty-five attempting conception are successful, and the spontaneous abortion rate at thirty-eight is double what it is in one's twenties, and triple in one's forties.[4] However, says Dr. Soderstrom, a woman in good health in her early forties who has no age-related conditions such as hypertension or adult-onset diabetes; who during her life has not contracted sexually transmitted diseases, severe pelvic inflammatory disease, or acute endometriosis; and who has no anatomical barriers to fertility, should not experience significant problems in getting pregnant or carrying a healthy baby to term.

He does not discount the genetic or other prenatal environmental hazards: "We give all women over thirty the chart indicating exactly what the statistical chances of problems are," he said. "If a woman has no religious or ethical strictures that would prohibit an abortion if the fetus turns out to be damaged, she can locate herself on that chart and decide whether or not to take the risk."

"I can't choose not to choose much longer," Laura said. "If I decide against it, I want to know that that was an active decision, not a passive one. I don't want to wake up a few years from now and wonder why I still don't have something I've always wanted—not when the answer is, because I just let it happen."

As I write this, Laura calls, and we agree to have lunch. Over the scampi, she tells me she has made a decision. "I found someone who agreed to help me out," she said. "And at the last minute, I decided I couldn't go through with it. It's simply too big a decision to make on behalf of an unborn child." She took a month's leave of absence, during which she traveled extensively in Third World countries. "There are so many babies and children who desperately need a parent out there," she said. "I was very locked into the idea of having my own until I saw them. And then I realized how little that really matters. It isn't who gives birth to a baby that counts—it's who loves it, nurtures it, teaches it." After weeks of red tape, a baby has been located; Laura is leaving on Friday for Colombia to bring her home, and her scampi gets cold as she discusses, with animation and excitement, the changes that are coming in her life. "I can hardly wait," she says, and on the way home, I stop in at the Carriage Trade, for the second time this month, to buy a gift for a child who has found a home with a single woman who wants to give it a future.

MOTHERING A CHILD OR REPARENTING YOURSELF?

A few years ago, when my daughter was having a raging case of adolescence, I sighed wearily and said to no one in particular, "I've been thirteen once—why do I have to go through it again?" And Jenny told me. "When you were my age, did you ever say to yourself, 'When I have a kid, I'll be a different kind of mother than my mother is? I won't get mad, I won't go power tripping, I'll really understand'?" Yes, I nodded, I'd felt that way—once. "Well, unless you're willing to be thirteen again, at least in your head, you can't," said my infuriatingly accurate kid.

Single or not, when we consider being mothers, both Small and Big Minds remember the mothers and fathers we had. If what they gave us wasn't enough, was the wrong thing, at the wrong time, in the wrong way, we believe we can rewrite our past by changing the present. At the conscious level, we may believe we have come to terms with whatever we lost, or never had to begin with: love, understanding, acceptance, a feeling of importance, or even just adequacy. It may not be our own mothers' mistakes or lacks we are trying to compensate for; many single mothers in one recent study reported good relationships with their maternal parents, but troubled, distant, negative connections with their fathers.[5] If their fathers were emotionally or actually absent during their childhoods, they may be seeking to replicate that experience in the present by raising their own children in fatherless homes.

The urge to have and live in a family assumes overwhelming importance to the adult, especially if it wasn't fulfilled in childhood. But so does it for those whose emotional needs were met: Says Kathleen, "I had a wonderful, wonderful, childhood. Both my parents gave so much of themselves. It's that situation I want to repeat, not a miserable one." The death of Kathleen's mother brought to the fore her unsatisfied longings for a child: "I just plain miss her so much," she sighs. "I think of all the things she taught me, all the wonderful stuff we did together, all her marvelous qualities. It would be a terrible loss not to pass those on to another child."

Marylou's experience was different; she had a troubled relationship with her recently deceased mother. "Now that she's dead, maybe I can get her voice out of my head," she said. "The voice of the judge, the critic, the one for whom I was never good enough, or always doing something wrong. Maybe having a child would allow me to replace that negative voice with a positive one—my own. By becoming the kind of mother I didn't have, perhaps I can get free of the one I did."

Is it legitimate to attempt to meet emotional needs of that kind through a child? Having a child engenders the possibility that you can become a copy of your own mother, for good or for ill; by carrying and bearing a child, you become, in one sense, "the primary figure of [your] internal being, replacing the internalized mother with [your] own enhanced self."[6]

Many who think about having a child, partnered or alone, have a sense that this time, they can "do it right." That feeling may not even be related to childhood experience; it may simply be that we are wiser than we once were, that we know things we didn't then. Although I've had my kids, every twenty-eight days I think, however fleetingly, about having another—because this time, I believe (once again, the triumph of hope over experience), I could "do it right." And until we are parents ourselves, it is hard to understand, and hence forgive, the parents who failed us in some way. Until that time, we may sense but not truly know that whatever our parents did wrong, most of them didn't do so because they were inherently cruel, angry, or abusive; they simply didn't know any better. Their motivation, like ours, was love— misplaced or misguided, perhaps, but love nonetheless.

TELLING YOURSELF THE TRUTH
Women who are thinking about having children on their own tell or enact a number of untruths—to themselves as well as to others. One of these is about why they want a child. Another is when. And a third is how.

Some women deliberately select a particular father and wage a campaign. It may be because they achingly want a child; it may also be because the relationship is ending and they want to prolong it or have something to remember it by; or because a lover refuses to be pinned down by any other means; or because they see him as their last chance for motherhood. If they "need" to be in love in order to rationalize having a child alone, they will often arrange to "fall" in love; they may not be hoping to marry the man, but want to be able to tell their child, some day, that they had a relationship of mutual caring that resulted in its conception. Women who choose to conceive by AI, however, have anticipated that need, and figured out a way to deal with that situation when it arises. Writes Jean Renvoize in *Going Solo: Single Mothers by Choice,* "Artificial insemination is making the clearest possible statement that I'm doing this completely alone; it's not an accident, I'm not a woman abandoned by a man, I am an independent, capable woman making a choice that is entirely my responsibility and no one else's, thank you very much."[7]

Although they may not admit it, some women choosing single motherhood are seeking escape from a troubled area of their life. They may be feeling stale and bored at work, in a stuck place in a relationship, overcome by spite at a lover who's left them, envious of a pregnant sister, eager to dispel the belief that they are dried-up career women who are too sexless to attract a lover. Others emphatically deny that their decision is related to what their friends and peers are doing. But when they reflect on it, they often admit what they are then able to see is the truth—or some part of it. Said Gena, "I never felt OK when I didn't have a boyfriend. Then, when I had one, that part of me didn't change; I still didn't feel entirely OK. I got into therapy and realized it was my inner life, not my outer one, that was hanging me up, making me feel abnormal in some way. I went to a counselor because I was starting to think, *If I had a child, I'd be normal—like everyone else.*"

Another way some women delude themselves is in the manner they choose to have a child. They "invite" accidents—they let their bodies decide, when it's their minds that are already made up. "What does 'by choice' really mean, anyway?" asked Leila, who now admits that that was what she did. "Choices can be made, rationally or irrationally. They can be acknowledged after the fact. They can be conscious or unconscious. What matters is that you recognize what kind yours was, and accept and validate it. Otherwise, you'll always be conflicted about it. My first choice was to have a baby with a man I loved, who wanted to have a baby with me. What I'm living with is my second choice, and it's just fine that way, now that I know that's what it is."

And there are women whose truths are so embedded in delusion or even lies that they cannot extricate themselves. "I wanted a baby, but I wasn't prepared to have it as an unmarried woman," said Nancy. "In fact, that's just what I did, although I told everyone, including my parents, that I was actually married. I invented a man—he existed, they even met him once, but we only had a couple of dates before he went back to Ireland, where he lived—and while my parents were on a round-the-world cruise, I later told them, I married and divorced him. By the time they came back I was eight months pregnant. I've told that story to so many people that I almost believe it myself now."

WHAT YOU GIVE AND WHAT YOU GET

Intentional single motherhood among middle-class women is still a relatively new phenomenon, so it may be too early to judge both the quality of the experience and its effect on the children involved. "Ask me on a Monday morning, and I'll tell you it was a big mistake," says Daisy, who had Max when she was thirty and unmarried. "Would I advise another woman to do it? Definitely not. Max and I weren't a family—until he was about nine or ten, what we were was a struggle." But most experts believe that children raised in happy homes by satisfied parents do not suffer particularly because their mothers are single. It is the mother's pleasure in her role and satisfaction that she is doing an adequate job as a parent that makes the difference. The reality of single parenthood depends to a great extent on whether or not it is voluntary. "Single parenthood is like greatness," says a divorced mother ruefully. "Some are called by it and others have it thrust upon us." One advantage of intentional single parenthood is that it is not necessary to compromise with another person on your ideas for raising children; another is that neither your happiness nor your child's is marred by the mess of a divorce or the unhappy memory of a bad relationship with the child's father. But all single mothers, divorced or never married, agree that without the help and support of a close-knit, caring community of friends and family, they never could have managed. The most political among the unmarried mothers I know are quick to remind me that the nuclear family—the monogamous couple with a child—is not the norm in every culture, class, or race. "The extended family and support network is a much older pattern," says Jennifer, an anthropologist who is herself a single mother. "What we see as normal in this culture is not necessarily the most typical pattern of the human race, even today. But I wouldn't advise any woman to have a child alone unless she can bring herself to reach out to others and ask for help, because she'll certainly need it. If she's militant about proving that she can do it all on her own, she'll be disappointed, because she simply cannot, no matter how smart or capable she is, how much money she has—although, of course, money helps a great deal. But if a woman persists in trying to be a Super-Self-Sufficient-I-Don't-Need-Anyone's-Help Single Mother, she and her child will both suffer."

LEE—WITH A LITTLE HELP FROM MY FRIENDS

A few years ago I opened my mail and found a meeting notice, complete with agenda. It was perfectly typed, grammatically correct—where did Lee get her new secretary, I wondered? And then I read it carefully and laughed and laughed. Lee—disorganized, distractable, often discombobulated Lee—was pregnant, and calling in her markers. As she told me later, "All of you who said, 'If you do it, we'll help you'—I was just taking you up on it."

The agenda was a marvel of careful planning. Next to each item, there was a request for whomever felt most capable of providing what it entailed to "volunteer." Let's see, I thought—*Do I want to be responsible for getting the crib, finding the nanny, finishing the extra bathroom, handling the layette, or being the Lamaze coach?*

Lee, who was forty-one then, had listed all the requirements she thought needed to be satisfied in order for her to have the baby she was carrying. She had had several abortions while in her twenties; at the time she wrote the memo, she'd been in a relationship for five years with a man who was neither interested in nor ready to have a baby. "When I would bring it up, he'd say, 'Sure, sure,' and then we wouldn't talk about it," Lee said. "On my forty-first birthday, I said, 'If I'm ever going to do it, I have to do it now,' and he said, 'Sure, sure,' again. When I got pregnant, six weeks later, he was at first surprised—he's six years younger than I am, and he told me he didn't think, due to my age, I *could* get pregnant. When we found out I was, he was very angry. I thought he'd probably split, but I decided I wanted this baby—and with a little help from my friends, I could have it. Which is why I sent that memo. I figured if they weren't going to help, I'd better know it before it was too late to change my mind."

As we agreed at the "Baby Business Meeting" that took place a few weeks later in Lee's apartment, the memo made each of us reexamine those blithe assurances we'd been so free in handing out to all our friends and acquaintances who were considering having children on their own. And we knew, too, that the items on the agenda like the layette and the nanny were only the beginning; if Lee went through with this, and her lover abandoned her as she expected he would, we were going to be in it for the long haul.

You may choose to meet your needs to mother a child less directly than Lee did, and one of those ways may be making a commitment to someone else's child. As the single mother of two children who were fortunate enough to have my friends in their lives, I can truly say that without that help, I couldn't have done it. Your commitment to be there for another's child may be casually made, but shouldn't be casually kept. And if you put in the time, effort, and energy to help someone else be a parent, you will be rewarded in the here as well as in the after by the friendship, company, and caring of a child who holds you in a special place in his heart simply because you're you. You don't *have* to be there for him, and he knows it. You're not his mother; maybe you're his godmother or aunt, or perhaps your affiliation is less formal, but you're there because you want to be. And what's in it for you? Not just being "my mother, once removed," as my daughter once described her relationship to my best friend, but having the opportunity and satisfaction of giving a gift to the future. At a certain point in our lives, most of us will feel that obligation to posterity. Whether you fulfill it by parenting your own child, or parenting another's, the reward is worth the price.

THE LONELY AND THE BRAVE

The woman who chooses to have a child alone doesn't want to make the one thing she can do that a man cannot do dependent on him. She wants a child intensely, and the degree of that intensity is measured by her unwillingness to wait for someone to give it to her. She has considered her motivation carefully and determined that being a mother on her own terms is a positive act. Her self-definition is clear; her decision is not the result of an identity crisis, and she is not choosing this particular means of proving her femininity. There is a reasonable congruence between her expectations of what she can offer a child and what is actually true. She feels loved, valued, good about herself, and satisfied with her life; her basic emotional needs have been satisfied in other ways. She doesn't underestimate the importance of a father to a child, but believes that even without one, her child can have a happy, productive life. She doesn't feel that she's making any major sacrifices on behalf of a child; thus, she will not burden it with that kind of emotional baggage. She is ready to move on to a new stage in life without being married or partnered. She has confidence in her coping abilities. She has a strong, secure personal support network, is financially solvent, and knows she can handle the economic responsibility that comes with parenthood.

She may have been a Sleeping Beauty once upon a time, but she has waited long enough for the child she desires. The awakened Sleeping Beauty knows how, when, and why to claim her dream herself.

❀ 9 ❀

Taking Chances, Risking Change

Only the assurance that no one would mistake the chic, confident woman I've become for the girl I was at twenty allowed me to even consider attending my college reunion. Spurred by Joan Didion's axiom that it is the duty of every writer to go to her reunion at least once, I prepared by unearthing my old Annual, and rereading the flowery couplets, clever quotations, smartass comments, and protestations of undying friendship penned across the class pictures. They all asked the same thing—that I never change, and they promised that they wouldn't, either.

Back then, I couldn't wait for change. After graduation, I hoped, I would shed my imperfect self, like a butterfly emerging from a cocoon, shake off the dust of my boring, bourgeois past (can a twenty-year-old be said to *have* a past?) and magically metamorphose into a totally new person. In another place I would reinvent myself for strangers who knew nothing of my undistinguished history, who had never laid eyes on me before I grew into the beauty I still hoped was in the offing, acquired the husband and family through whom I would fulfill my destiny, and achieved the pinnacle of literary glory.

Change has a funny habit of arriving in disguise; sometimes you don't notice you've traveled any distance until you look back and see how far you've come. I ignored my reunion notices for twenty years, until I felt as though the roads I'd taken had led to a place I was happy to be in. The geography of my life is not just where I've been, but where I haven't. So when my erstwhile classmates, most of whom I hadn't seen since graduation, proclaimed that I hadn't changed a bit, I was surprised. It wasn't the physical differences they ignored—by tacit agreement, we all skimmed lightly over those. But when they looked, they saw past those and through me, to that part of me—that part of all of us—that is all but immutable, that clings to a familiar set of values, beliefs, and behavior with the tenacity of a bulldog. It is that self, which I call the Keeper, that buffers us from the threatening winds of change and reassures us that, regardless of the passage of years and the accumulation of experience, we are who we were. Despite how different I thought I was from the girl I had been, my classmates still knew me. And, in a way I couldn't have predicted, I found that comforting.

While the Keeper inside us would like things to stay just the way they are (which is not to say that they couldn't be improved on here and there—couldn't they always?), the seductive voice of the Seeker is always tempting us into the unknown. Sometimes we welcome the Seeker, as most of us did when we were in college. At other times we fear it and try to ignore it, because the Seeker calls out for change. Change means taking risks, and sometimes accepting loss—loss of the real as well as the illusory. Change means giving up something we have for something we might not get. Change means motion. Change is the current of life's river, and occasionally it tumbles us into a maelstrom. But sometimes it leads us toward new and exciting landscapes.

The Keeper and the Seeker both guide us through the familiar passages of adulthood: leaving home, setting up a life on our own, choosing a career and forging intimate connections. While the Seeker inspires us to change, the Keeper reaffirms that part of us never will. Both aspects of self can help maintain our emotional balance. But fear of change can hold us back, even when the odds are that change will be for the better.

Change, whether we welcome it or not, is a fact of life. It can be minimal or major, as easy as cutting your hair or as difficult as ending a relationship. At every point along that continuum, both the Keeper and the Seeker have truths to teach: The Keeper knows that change means a potentially frightening adjustment to the new, but the Seeker knows that change invites growth. At different times in our lives, we may hear one voice more clearly than the other.

WHEN CHANGE EQUALS CHOICE

Some people resist change; others welcome it. And then there are those who require a constant diet of it. "Change junkies" never seem to be satisfied with what they have—a job, a lover, or a lifestyle. Some are consumers of commitment who casually jettison friends, lovers, careers, and aspirations on the assumption or even the remote possibility that something better or more significant is always just around the next bend in the river. Often they're *avoiding* growth by changing rather than evolving *through* change.

It is easier to embrace change and make it work for you when you see yourself as the agent rather than the victim of change—when you're free to decide for yourself how, where, and with whom you work, love, and live, what you want and what you get. If the changes you make in your life reflect deeply felt goals and desires, then the stress that accompanies them is minimal, and can even be positive. Between the terror over change that many women experience and the chronic dissatisfaction they feel about their lives *as they are* lies a middle ground where the Keeper and the Seeker can meet.

Resisting change may help us avoid discomfort, departures, and even failure. But it also closes the door to joy, delight, and arrival. We can make some kinds of changes less frightening by planning carefully and trying things out one step at a time. We can take care not to burden change with unrealistic expectations. And we can arm ourselves against disappointment by visualizing what the worst thing that could happen might be, and knowing that even if it happens, we will survive it.

Change is a risky but rewarding venture that begins with the questions: What is there in your life that you value, and what is missing from it?

MIRA—HOW MUCH "JAM" IS ENOUGH?

Mira wasn't at her best the night we met. Earlier that day the bow on her blouse didn't droop, her hair hadn't lost its moussey lift, her nose wasn't shiny, and the rings under her eyes weren't so dark. Earlier that day she'd been smart but not threatening, self-possessed but not cocky, feminine but not wishy-washy, assertive but not aggressive—all the things a working woman has to be these days. Earlier that day her feet didn't hurt so much and Mira didn't know she wouldn't get home until well after midnight because the fog had rolled in to blanket the runways and her plane was going to be at least an hour late.

She had cornered the last table in the terminal cocktail lounge, and I didn't want to intrude, but my plane was delayed too and there was nowhere else to sit. So I thanked her in a way that I hoped let her know that I knew what a nice person she was being and collapsed into the chair across from her.

I have this game I play with myself when I'm traveling, trying to figure out who people are by the only clues you get from strangers. I notice what they're wearing, reading, carrying, their body language, accent and manner, even whether they tip carefully or carelessly or if their American Express cards are green or gold. I construct entire lives for them, because I'm a journalist who also writes novels, and when they get up and walk out of my life I think I know them, even if we've never exchanged a word. This woman across from me wore no rings—she's either single or divorced, I thought, in her mid-thirties. I could tell from the business card in the plastic window of her Daytimer that she worked for a computer company on the East Coast, from the tag on her carry-on that she spent her last vacation in Paris. I assumed, from the books that she'd tucked into the bag's outside pocket, that she wasn't happy with her job and had recently broken up with a lover; everyone I knew who was thinking about changing careers or having an unhappy love affair was reading those books that year. What her tags, labels, and book titles didn't tell me my imagination colored in, the outlines and texture of an unknown woman's life. And when the loudspeaker announced another delay, we exchanged shrugs the way people do in those situations, and began to talk. We traded a few carefully edited pieces of our history and took each other's measure. By the time the fog finally lifted, three hours later, we boarded the plane together. When we disembarked at the opposite end of the country, in the city where Mira lived and I had business, I'd accepted her invitation to dinner a few days later.

Her address turned out to be a crumbling three-story Victorian on a block where shiny new BMWs were parked next to the rusting bodies of stripped, abandoned cars. Light and sound spilled from the windows of her house; inside, I made my way through and around a dozen people before I found Mira, who explained that she shared the house with three of them: George, who owns a hair salon; Peggy, a single mother; and Drindy, Peggy's teenage daughter. One floor at a time, they are renovating the house. Mira lives on the top floor, which has a bird's-eye view of Boston harbor. That night she was having a party to celebrate the completion of her apartment.

It all seemed like a television sitcom, the characters right out of central casting, today's version of the nuclear family: a gay man, a straight woman, a single parent, and a teenager, gentrifying a house in an inner-city neighborhood. After the last guest had departed, Mira and I put our feet up with a brandy and settled down to talk.

"I never expected to be a spinster. That's what it says on my mortgage papers; that's the language some banks still use when it's a single woman buying a house. Can you imagine?" Mira chuckled. She bought the house three years ago, after breaking up with her longtime lover. "It didn't make sense to throw my money away on rent any longer. But once I bought it, it was simply too much for me. I was really stretched financially. The house is almost a hundred years old, so something's always falling apart. I'd be in Texas or California on a sales trip, sitting in my hotel room listening to Willard Scott saying it was pouring buckets in Boston, and be worrying about whether my roof was leaking. Or I'd want something like a new car, and realize that I couldn't afford it anymore. And in the first year I was broken into and ripped off three times when I was away. So I began to be scared about living here alone. That was when I decided to rent out the other floors. But they were still such a mess that I couldn't charge enough rent to make it worthwhile. Peggy was first—she said she'd do some of the repairs in exchange for a reduction in rent. Then George moved in on the same basis. It worked out so well we decided to become financial partners. Their sweat equity was their down payment. They've stayed not just because it's a good investment, but because it's turned into a good way to live for all of us."

A few months ago Mira refinanced the house with the help of her new partners. They formed a company to restructure owner-ship. "I showed Peggy and George my original mortgage, where it said 'spinster,' and we were hysterical," said Mira. "George thought the new papers should say, 'the spinster, the faggot, and the failure.' Society's rejects, he calls us. So that's our company name—the SR Company. Did you notice the monogrammed tow-els in the bathroom?"

Mira had wanted a house for a long time. "All my life, really," she said. "There were six of us, plus my folks, and my grand-mother, who lived with us till she was eighty, and I never had a room I didn't have to share. I also hated the way my mother kept things—the plastic on the couch, the doilies on the chairs, the artificial flowers and the saints' pictures—yecch! I used to clip pictures out of magazines when I was a kid, the way I wanted my home to be someday."

Mira first found the house with her fiancé—"We were going to buy it together, and when we broke up, I decided to do it on my own. I mortgaged myself to the hilt, which meant that I had no freedom to change careers, which I was also thinking of doing. Up until then, for about ten years after I finished school, I was just putting in my hours. Doing a job I was good at, but bored with. Going to a lot of singles' places. Hotels in the mountains, Club Med. My girlfriends all got married and I felt really alone, especially after I broke my engagement. I think I went to those places because I had no home. I had this dinky overpriced apartment in a fancy part of town, but it wasn't really a home."

What she has now has turned out to be more than just a house for Mira. "I have some really special people in my life I didn't have before. George and Peggy and Drindy. We take care of each other. Sometimes it's a pain, especially when one of us is depressed, but we respect each other's boundaries. Drindy is a bonus—she's a major part of my life. She's probably the closest I'll ever have to a child, and that's OK now—I see what Peggy goes through, the worry and the responsibility, and I'm not sure I could handle that alone. Even if I got married and had a kid with someone, there's no guarantee I wouldn't be doing it mostly myself someday. And besides, I don't like babies, I like older kids."

Maybe when Drindy goes to college, Mira will adopt one. It's a possibility she never considered until now. But first she wants to finish renovating the house, put in a garden, and pay down the mortgage. And that's not all. There's a group of women at her gym who are going to raft the Colorado River this summer, and she wants to do that, too. And she's looking for a job that doesn't require as much travel as the one she has now; letting a job take over her whole life, says Mira, is unhealthy. "At a certain point, there's nothing in it except money. Once you have enough to make you feel secure, why break your neck?" She'd put more energy into her job if she thought there was anything more to get out of it. Since there doesn't seem to be, she's starting to look into other possibilities. "I always wanted to be a designer, only I went into computers because of the money. But what I really want to be is an interior designer, and I think I've figured out how to combine them into one thing, which would be more entrepreneurial—I'd have to start my own business. That's only a dream right now, even though I'm taking night courses in design and business management. Going back to school at my age is hard, but there's a different quality to the experience when you're an adult. You're not trying to just coast through, you want to do it well enough to justify the commitment and live up to your own idea of what you're capable of. It really stretches you."

So do the intimate connections Mira's made with the friends who have become her family. "George's lover died last year. We all went through his illness together. Through that I became involved with an outreach group that helps AIDS patients," Mira said. "Their strength and courage has really taught me a lot. It's deepened my life. It's made me determined to live every day as if it were my last, which is not something I ever thought much about until recently."

Mira's had one serious love affair since she bought her house, "and about a million blind dates," she adds. "I date when there's someone interesting to go out with. When there's not, I can usually get someone here to go to a movie or do something. What I miss most is steady sex—anything casual is taking your life in your hands. I don't think I've slept with a man for over a year now. But on the whole, my life is much better now that I'm past the craziness of having to be with a man all the time. If someone showed up and said, 'Let me take you away from all this,' I'd probably laugh in his face—now that's a big change in me. Any guy would have to understand from the git-go that I need a certain degree of independence. And of course, he'd have to love George and Peggy and Drindy, too."

Mira tossed another log in the crackling fire in her cozy living room and stretched all five feet plenty of her strong, muscular body. "Did you ever have one of those periods in your life when you had everything you wanted, and you thought, *If I could only keep it this way, hold onto this moment?* When you think to yourself, *Girl, this is happiness and don't you forget it?* Well, that's what this is. One of those times. I used to say, "All I need is enough jam.""

J.A.M., you know? The right Job, the right Apartment, the right Man. The sweetness you put on whatever slice of life you're living at a given time. It's funny—I don't have at least two of those things right now, and life is sweeter than it's ever been."

These days Mira thinks more about what she'd have to give up to get married than about what she'd gain. "Not that I think about it all that often to begin with," she said. "Mostly it happens when I go somewhere with my married friends, and think, *Oh, yeah, wouldn't that be nice.* And then they say to me, 'Oh, Mira, I wish I had your life.' So I guess the grass is always greener."

WHAT HAVE YOU GOT TO LOSE?

Fear holds us back from change, even when change is what we need. My friend Tory has been in a dead-end job for years. It's not due to lack of opportunity—she's a talented sportswear designer who's been courted by the top companies in her field. Loyalty to the boss who gave her her first real break keeps Tory from making the move that's necessary to advance her career. Marvin takes her designs and changes only her initials in the lower righthand corner. He keeps raising her salary, a few dollars at a time, but he refuses to give her credit. She's been offered enough financing to start her own label, money that would bankroll her for at least two seasons. But the Keeper's voice so dominates Tory's view of who she is, and what she can be, that she can't hear the Seeker.

JoEllen, a social worker who's thirty-four now, detests change. As a child, she never went to the same school more than two years in a row. Her father was in the military service, and when he got orders, they went. Every time she had to say good-bye to friends—or, even harder, try to make new ones somewhere else— she vowed that once she could control her life, she'd never move again. The happiest year of her adolescence was her fifteenth, when she fell in love with the boy next door in the town her family lived in then. They were transferred elsewhere the year later, but when JoEllen was ready for college, she came back. When she graduated, she took a job less than ten miles from the campus and married her high school sweetheart. She values stability over everything else, and although she was divorced after eight years of marriage, nothing else has changed in her life. That's the way she wants it. She was powerless to resist the traumatic changes of her youth so she's arranged her life, insofar as possible, to keep change at bay as best she can.

Marilyn, who endured a major upheaval when she was a child—her father died suddenly and her mother remarried a man who abused her—has reason to be frightened of change, too. But that early experience didn't keep her, at thirty-one, from walking out of a bad marriage, even though, as her mother told her, she had "everything a woman could want," including a new house, a Mercedes, vacations in Europe, and designer clothes. She had worked as a nurse before she was married; her husband, a doctor, thought one career in the family was enough. "When I realized how much I was giving up—not his money, but my life—I left," she said. "My choice was clear." While Marilyn's Seeker instigated change, her Keeper kept her emotionally afloat while she actually did it, reminding her that her basic goals and values—the *real* Marilyn—hadn't changed.

What change leaves behind are ideas about one's self that, like outgrown clothes, no longer fit: attitudes, roles, and even limitations you once thought you were stuck with. Carol, who faced a life-threatening illness just as the life she'd planned was beginning to unroll in front of her like a red-velvet carpet, couldn't back away from change. Some of her dreams died very hard, but she handled it with grace, humor, and courage that made all her friends marvel. Her mother died when she was only forty, and ever since, Carol thought that she would, too, although until she became ill, with a totally unrelated disease, there was no reason to think so. "In order to survive, it was necessary to let go of that belief. In order to face the future, I had to assume that I'd have one," she said. "An experience like that changes you in a very elemental way. When I reached the age my mother was when she died, I knew I was going to live forever. Well, not forever," she added, "but fully and completely, as long as I do."

MID-LIFE CRISIS OR REASONABLE RISK?

There comes a time in every woman's life when the dreams of the past are held up to the mirror of the present; when whatever is left on that Life List of long ago—whatever still matters—begins to trouble her thoughts, disturb her dreams, interrupt what she's doing, even if she's perfectly satisfied to be doing it, as I was.

I don't remember now which came first, the need or the fantasy. I knew only that I was stale. Bored. In a rut. Those are lifeless words, evocative of exactly how I felt then: without aliveness. There was no one dramatic event that precipitated the emotion, just fatigue from having weathered the predictable passages to adulthood. Embarrassingly stereotypical, this mid-life crisis, but I was stuck with it. My life had the essential ingredients of satisfaction: enjoyable, productive work, pleasing and comfortable surroundings, intimate human connections. What it lacked was the anticipation of joy—the feeling that maybe today, something wonderful would happen. Or at least something different.

The time had come to make a change. To take a risk. To move, if only for the sake of motion. To hold entropy and inertia at bay. Yet I hesitated; I decorated my rut with new furnishings, but it was still the same old rut.

In it was a network of friends and habits and routines that had once felt nurturing and supportive but now seemed inhibiting. I was tired of myself; I wanted to invent a new life. My delicate cobweb of necessary connections had become a trap. If I deviated from expected, established ways of being, I might threaten or even destroy what I had so carefully constructed.

In that rut, too, were other things I valued: a house that I had made a home; a sense of self and place that was inextricably aligned with my personal identity. There was nothing really wrong, with me or with my life—but the sum had become less than the total of its parts. I began to consider moving across the country.

I didn't think a major relocation would make a significant difference to my career. The beauty of my work is that it is portable; I can do it anywhere. What I lacked was not opportunity but energy; it seemed that I'd used it up in the city that had been my home for almost twenty years. New York, which beckoned me, was professionally (as well as every other way) a much more competitive milieu. Up to that point I had done well enough without ever really testing myself against my peers. It occurred to me that there were career benefits in moving. But that, too, was too bold an expectation for such a fragile fantasy. My goals remained hazy and blurred.

There was no plausible man in my life, and many of my friends thought that my tentative plan to uproot myself and move some three thousand miles away was connected with that state of affairs. Of course, I had considered it, but if the Prince had not found me in a city of a half million, how likely was it that he'd discover me in one with nine million? I tried very hard not to overburden my almost formless plans with expectations of that nature.

The trade-offs involved in such a move came in for the greatest scrutiny. I wasn't prepared to sacrifice my friends for my career; I was willing to be the most flexible about my surroundings. I had worked hard to buy and fix up my house, and I loved it; it was clear from the outset that I couldn't hope to live as well in a much more expensive city. Still, the pleasure I took in my house was dimming a bit—yes, that's what I'd give up, if something had to be given up. The possessions of a life can be left or lent; the accumulated responsibilities of adulthood—friends for one, family for another—are not so easily put aside. They were proof that I had passed beyond the carefree point where all that's necessary to pick up stakes is a backpack and a cheerful wave good-bye.

Characteristically, I do big things in small steps; I rarely lift a foot until it's clear just where and how firmly it can be put down again. Parameters are necessary; to me, too much freedom is anarchy. Or, at the very least, alienation. So one summer I tried out that new life in Manhattan, and returned home in September with the answers to some important questions. Having learned that I could make new friends—good friends, close friends—and that I could support myself, I saw that, if I did things carefully and planned them well, my center would hold.

Now there was shape and texture to my hazy fantasy, although I still would not have said that relocating, starting a new life somewhere else, was a goal. It seemed pretentious, and in it lurked the possibility of failure. Yet I put money into a savings account, strengthened the professional connections I made during the summer, and cultivated friendships I'd begun in New York with letters, phone calls, and brief return visits.

In the two and a half years between thinking about change and making it happen, I was often terribly frightened. Then I sabotaged myself, like someone who fasts for a week and then binges on frozen chocolate chip cookie dough. My version of binging was a financial mess that could easily have been prevented. Cleaning it up postponed my departure for nearly a year. So did an unsuitable suitor to whom I clung, half hoping he would say the words that would provide me with an excuse not to do what I knew I needed to do. To move is to risk dying, my Keeper warned; not to move is to be dead already, my Seeker replied.

I spent sleepless nights categorizing disaster scenarios. I remembered a man I knew who had planned an odyssey around the world for several years. He'd scrimped for it, saved for it, sold his house, cut his ties, left his friends and his lover. Ten days after he departed he returned, with the simple explanation that the planning had been more satisfying than the doing. As soon as he got to a strange place, he told me, he realized that he wanted to be in a familiar one, so he just came home. I marveled at his courage—not in leaving, but in returning.

I stayed in New York as long as I'd planned to, and my disaster scenarios never materialized. Instead, I found a new fantasy, had a new idea, set a new goal, and saw that the first change had merely been preparation for the others that would follow. That's one of the benefits of making a change, living a fantasy—it opens up the possibility of others.

What remained of that year was the knowledge that it is possible to seize control of one's life and shape it to fit one's fantasy. The act of risking, of moving, is its own reward; the exhilaration has its own momentum. For a few years thereafter, my energies were divided between two different lives in two different places. I found that I had twice as much, with rewards and possibilities in both. Before that, I'd been bored and understimulated; afterward, I was overstimulated and sometimes frazzled. Before, my mind was rusty, my emotional affect flat, my career at a dead end; after, it all seemed just slightly more than I could handle. But what was missing in my life had returned—that hoped-for joy. It didn't arrive every day, but it appeared on occasion. And in between there was newness, a changed perspective, a constant aliveness that comes from change itself.

My journey was greater than all of its miles, which is what change is about—just as a rut is about feeling that there is no choice, no possibility of change. Even the most comfortable rut can seem like a room with no windows, a circle closed in on itself.

Friends tell me of their ruts. Dinah's rut is a marriage that isn't dreadful or tragic, but it's not happy, either. Maribeth's is a constant state of indebtedness that ensures that there will be no way for her to make tomorrow different from today. Pat's is a job that is secure, but routine and unrewarding.

Other people recount dramatic and spontaneous acts—walking out on jobs, families, lovers, and lives without even a fantasy, much less a direction. Some of them seem to manage quite well; perhaps their capacity for risking everything is greater than mine. Or maybe they value what is good and rewarding in their existence so little that they can leave it without a tear or a backward glance. Some are commitment consumers, leaving the ones they've made in the vague hope that a better one will turn up.

Because the only promise I had to keep was to myself, I was free to risk, to initiate a process that began with a reassessment, with these questions: What was there in my life that I treasured, and what was missing from it? The question provided the answer, the direction, and suggested the steps along the way.

"It'll all be different when you come back," a friend sighed when I told her of my plan. "*If* you come back," she added darkly. "It will all be changed."

Of course it would be. For change, Sleeping Beauty, is exactly the point.

❈ 10 ❈

Creating a Life on Paper and Living It in the World; a Fairy Tale

O nce upon a time, there was a Princess. Maybe no one else knew she was a Princess; maybe she'd been banished from the castle by the King's jealous wife.

Or maybe everyone knew she was a Princess, but after she fell into that long sleep, people forgot. And by the time she woke up, no one remembered. Including her. She had a tension headache, and the feeling that she'd forgotten something very important, but she didn't know exactly what it was. Just a . . . feeling.

She looked at her watch, the one the King gave her on her sixteenth birthday, with the Magic Perpetual Calendar, and saw that a few years had elapsed. She hadn't a clue as to where she'd been all that time. All her friends were away, except the married ones with children; they couldn't get a baby-sitter. And even if they could, they didn't have a lot of free time.

When she got to the office, no one even noticed she'd been away. It was like she'd been there at her desk every morning for the last umpty-ump years, although she knew she hadn't. The mail in her In Box was dated a long time ago.

When she came home after work, someone had leveled the castle and put up a fancy new building. They told her because she had tenant's rights, she could get an insider price on one of the penthouse apartments, but she couldn't afford to buy it.

It occurred to Princess that if she didn't do something soon—anything—she'd be a very old, lonely, poverty-stricken woman. And she'd never have done anything much with her life. Nobody would ever have known she existed, except that old biddy who hadn't been invited to the christening and caused all Princess's trouble to begin with. She'd never have offered her gifts to the world, never have sampled the treasures of others'. She'd never have seen the kingdom's far corners, never have sampled the wines of its vineyards, never have dived in its deep azure seas. She'd never have known the delights of the body, rarely have ventured the depths of her soul.

Princess was overwhelmed by her vision. She fell into a despair so great, so wrenching, that even the taxi cabbies of the kingdom noticed; at least, they hollered "Hey, whyncha' watch where ya' goin, lady!" Her friends noticed, too—the ones who hadn't gone anywhere. They said, "Do a little something with your clothes—they're dreadfully out of date, where have you been all these years?" Her father said she was looking a little peaked.

Her doctor diagnosed a raging case of Statisticitis, complicated by DMS (Delayed Marriage Syndrome), and prescribed copious amounts of chocolate. She gave Princess one more refill of her antidepressant pills and went out of town to the Frozen Wasteland, where the odds on finding a mate with at least a sixth-grade education were said to be slightly higher. Her college roommate (the rich one) said that if Princess went on Oprah and told about her crippling affliction—until now, the Disease That Dared Not Speak Its Name—she could get it a charity gala all its own.

Princess's fairy godmother offered to pay for a face-lift, and her sister, who is rather stupid but married to a millionaire, gave her a week at a singles' club.

Princess said, "Thanks a lot, guys, but I think I can handle this. If *I* don't, nobody will. A year from now, nothing will have changed, except that a year will have passed."

So she thought and she thought, and then she took inventory.

She looked around at what she had—her life—and decided it wasn't enough. So she went out and got more. She knew you couldn't get more time, but you could always get more life.

It wasn't as easy as I'm making it sound—after all, she was only a Princess, and slightly imperfect at that. But she managed. She took care of the basics first: She found a better job, a decent place to live, and some new clothes. She made a few friends, and looked up some old ones. She got a library card, and a museum membership, and since she figured she might as well drop in on the Frozen Wasteland at least once—after all, now she knew someone there—she learned how to ski.

People noticed that Princess was smiling a lot more lately. And on the occasional day when she wasn't, they were especially nice to her, since it clearly wasn't a permanent condition. She began to notice them, too—especially men. Sometimes they smiled back at her and sometimes they didn't. It was always better when they did.

The weeks went by and then the months, and Princess wanted someone to snuggle with at night and play with during the day, so she got Schatzi (which means "a little darling" in the language of the kingdom). She taught Schatzi all the tricks she knew, shared all her deepest secrets, and loved Schatzi immensely. And Schatzi returned the favor.

One day a stranger knocked at her door. "Are you the Princess?" he asked. "Well, I'm *a* Princess. Who are you?" she said. "My name is Prince," he told her. "I hear you've been looking for me."

"No, you must have the wrong Princess," she said. "I've been extremely busy lately . . . wait, I think I *do* remember hearing about a Prince, a long time ago. Was that you?" He didn't look like the Prince she remembered, vaguely, from a long time ago. Not in that green jacket with those unfortunate little bumps all over it. "Well, look, you might as well come in," she said. "I've got a little time before I have to wash my hair tonight, so I suppose we could talk."

And they talked and they talked, and he came back often. She liked having him there. But when he was gone, she enjoyed that, too. She sort of liked being by herself—eating pizza at three in the morning was fun sometimes, and so was really digging into a project when she wanted to. And there was Schatzi to think of—the Prince was allergic to Schatzi.

Eventually they worked out a compromise. From Monday to Thursday Princess lived her own life, and on weekends she and the Prince were together. Except when they were apart, and that happened sometimes, because life is like that.

One day she passed an old crone in the street. She did a double-take; why, it was that awful woman who'd put the spell on her. Princess had forgotten all about her! She walked on, humming softly to herself, and somehow she felt lighter, happier. And this time, when she crossed against the light, lost in her pleasant reverie, the cabbie didn't run her over.

The Princess is all recovered from Statisticitis complicated by DMS now (or was it the other way around?). She threw away her copy of *Passive Women/Postponed Choices,* and forgave her parents for everything—even for letting her sleep all those years. Her latest book, *Passing as an Airhead: A Woman's Guide to Getting Married in the Nineties* is a huge success. She is the honorary president of a support group known as Statistics Anonymous, whose motto is, "It only takes one." Upon request, she will be happy to send you the name of the group nearest you.

Notes

CHAPTER ONE: TAKING YOURSELF OFF HOLD

[1] Carol Gilligan, *In a Different Voice: Psychological Theory and Women's Development* (Cambridge: Harvard University Press, 1982), p. 13.

[2] Dr. Charles M. Johnston, *The Creative Imperative* (Berkeley: Celestial Arts, 1984), p. 234.

[3] Faith Wilding, as quoted in Judy Chicago, *Through the Flower* (Garden City, N.Y.: Doubleday, 1975), pp. 213–217.

[4] Lisa Grunwald, "A Real Life Fairy Tale," *Esquire*, December 1988, p. 176.

[5] Ibid., p. 176ff.

CHAPTER TWO: TOO SMART FOR YOUR OWN GOOD

[1] Judith Guest, "The Mythic Family," the Thistle Series (Minneapolis: Milkweed Editions, 1988), p. 2.

[2] T. S. Eliot, *Four Quartets* (New York: Harcourt Brace, 1943), pp. 38–39.

CHAPTER THREE: A LIFE FOR YOURSELF

[1] As quoted in Maggie Scarf, *Unfinished Business* (New York: Ballantine, 1980), p. 37.

[2] M. Scott Peck, *The Road Less Traveled* (New York: Touchstone, 1978), p. 11.

[3] Daniel Levinson et al., *The Seasons of a Man's Life* (New York: Alfred A. Knopf, 1978), p. 163.

[4] Grace Baruch et al., *Lifeprints: New Patterns of Love and Work for Today's Women* (New York: New American Library, 1983), p. 261.

CHAPTER FOUR: GETTING DOWN TO BUSINESS

[1] Baruch et al., op. cit., p. 162.

[2] Quoting Pamela Daniels of the Wellesley College Center for Research on Women, ibid., p. 163.

Notes

[3] Janice LaRouche and Regina Ryan, *Strategies for Women at Work* (New York: Avon Books, 1984), p. 257.

[4] Baruch et al., op. cit., p. 35.

[5] *The Working Woman Success Book* (New York: Ace Books, 1981), p. 217.

CHAPTER FIVE: FRIENDSHIP IS A CATEGORY YOU INVENT YOURSELF

[1] Shirley Luthman, *Intimacy* (Los Angeles: Nash Publishing, 1972), p. 118.

[2] Letty Pogrebin, *Among Friends* (New York: McGraw-Hill, 1987), p. 145.

[3] Judith Viorst, *Necessary Losses* (New York: Fawcett, 1986), pp. 196–199.

[4] Pogrebin, op. cit., p. 8.

[5] Catherine Keller, *From a Broken Web* (Boston: Beacon Press, 1986), p. 17.

[6] Gerry Hirshey, "Coupledom Über Alles," *The Washington Post Magazine,* February 1988, quoted in *Utne Reader,* March/April 1989, p. 67.

[7] Rachel Kranz, "Toward a New Definition of Singleness," *Sojourner,* March 1986, quoted in *Utne Reader,* March/April 1989, pp. 70–74.

[8] Ibid., pp. 70–76ff.

[9] Ibid.

[10] Pogrebin, op. cit., p. 123.

[11] Guest, op. cit., p. 3.

[12] Madonna Kolbenschlag, *Lost in the Land of Oz: The Search for Identity and Community in American Life* (New York: Harper & Row, 1988), p. 9.

CHAPTER SIX: THE MAN/WOMAN CONNECTION

[1] Jane Wagner, *The Search for Signs of Intelligent Life in the Universe* (New York: Perennial, 1985), p. 34.

[2] Judith Sills, *How to Stop Looking for Someone Perfect and Find Someone to Love* (New York: Ballantine, 1984), p. 66.

[3] Erica Abeel, in *Hers: Through Women's Eyes,* ed. Nancy Newhouse (New York: Villard, 1985), p. 81.

[4] Linda Bird Francke, in ibid., p. 86.

[5] Sills, op. cit., p. 22.

[6] Ibid., p. 155.

[7] Mark Kramer, in Edward Klein, *About Men* (New York: Pocket Books, 1987), pp. 124–125.

[8] Michael Blumenthal, in ibid., p. 136.

[9] As quoted by Jane O'Reilly in "A Different Rapture," *Lear's,* March 1989, p. 159.

Notes

CHAPTER SEVEN: IF MONEY COULD BUY HAPPINESS, COULD YOU AFFORD IT?

[1] Edward M. Hallowell and William Grace, *What Are You Worth?* (New York: Weidenfeld & Nicholson, 1989), p. 40.
[2] Bruno Bettelheim, *The Uses of Enchantment* (New York: Vintage, 1987), p. 233.
[3] Michael Phillips, *The Seven Laws of Money* (Menlo Park, N.J.: Word Wheel Books and Random House, 1974), p. 67.
[4] Ibid., p. 170.

CHAPTER EIGHT: CATCH 35: DO YOU REALLY WANT A CHILD?

[1] Anita Micossi, "Just the Two of Us," *SAVVY*, September 1987, p. 43.
[2] Sharyne Merrit and Linda Steiner, *And Baby Makes Two* (New York: Franklin Watts, 1984), pp. 4–8.
[3] Jean Renvoize, *Going Solo: Single Mothers by Choice* (Boston: Routledge & Kegan Paul, 1985), p. 13.
[4] Marilyn Fabe, *Up Against the Clock* (New York: Warner Books, 1979), p. 72.
[5] Renvoize, op. cit., p. 132.
[6] Ibid., p. 24.
[7] Ibid., p. 189.

Bibliography

Baruch, Grace, Rosalind Barnett, and Caryl Rivers. *Lifeprints: New Patterns of Love and Work for Today's Women*. New York: Signet, 1983.

Belenky, Mary et al. *Women's Ways of Knowing*. New York: Basic Books, 1986.

Bettelheim, Bruno. *The Uses of Enchantment*. New York: Vintage, 1977.

Bolen, Jean. *Goddesses in Every Woman*. New York: Harper & Row, 1984.

Chicago, Judy. *Through the Flower*. Garden City, N.Y.: Doubleday, 1975.

Christ, Carol. *Diving Deep and Surfacing*. Boston: Beacon Press, 1980.

———. *The Laughter of Aphrodite*. New York: Harper & Row, 1987.

Davidson, Joy. *The Agony of It All*. Los Angeles: Tarcher, 1988.

Dowling, Colette. *Cinderella Complex*. New York: Summit, 1981.

Fabe, Marilyn. *Up Against the Clock*. New York: Warner Books, 1979.

Gilligan, Carol. *In a Different Voice: Psychological Theory and Women's Development*. Cambridge: Harvard University Press, 1982.

Guest, Judith. *The Mythic Family*. Minneapolis: Milkweed Editions, 1988.

Gurney, Kathleen. *Your Money Personality*. Garden City, N.Y.: Doubleday, 1988.

Hallowell, Edward M., and William Grace. *What Are You Worth?* New York: Weidenfeld & Nicholson, 1989.

Jaffee, Dennis. *Take This Job and Love It*. New York: Fireside, 1988.

Johnson, Robert. *Inner Work*. New York: Harper & Row, 1986.

Johnston, Charles M. *The Creative Imperative*. San Francisco: Celestial Arts, 1986.

Keller, Catherine. *From a Broken Web*. Boston: Beacon Press, 1986.

Klein, Edward, and Don Erickson. *About Men*. New York: Pocket Books, 1987.

Kolbenschlag, Madonna. *Kiss Sleeping Beauty Goodbye*. New York: Harper & Row, 1979.

———. *Lost in the Land of Oz*. New York: Harper & Row, 1988.

Lapham, Lewis. *Money & Class in America*. New York: Ballantine, 1988.

Bibliography

LaRouche, Janice, and Regina Ryan. *Strategies for Women at Work*. New York: Avon Books, 1984.

Levinson, Daniel. *The Seasons of a Man's Life*. New York: Alfred A. Knopf, 1978.

Littwin, Susan. *The Postponed Generation*. New York: William Morrow, 1986.

Luthman, Shirley. *Intimacy*. Los Angeles: Nash Publishing, 1972.

McLaughlin, Robert et al. *The Changing Lives of American Women*. Chapel Hill, North Carolina: University of North Carolina Press, 1988.

Margolies, Eva. *The Best of Friends, the Worst of Enemies*. New York: Pocket Books, 1985.

Merrit, Sharyne, and Linda Steiner. *And Baby Makes Two*. New York: Franklin Watts, 1984.

Merser, Cheryl. *GrownUps*. New York: New American Library, 1987.

McKaughan, Molly. *The Biological Clock*. New York: Penguin, 1987.

Miller, Alice. *The Drama of the Gifted Child*. New York: Basic Books, 1981.

Newhouse, Nancy, ed. *Hers: Through Women's Eyes*. New York: Villard, 1985.

Peck, M. Scott. *The Road Less Traveled*, New York: Touchstone, 1978.

Phillips, Michael. *The Seven Laws of Money*. New York: Random House, 1974.

Pogrebin, Letty. *Among Friends*. New York: McGraw-Hill, 1988.

Renvoize, Jean. *Going Solo: Single Mothers by Choice*. Boston: Routledge & Kegan Paul, 1985.

Richardson, Laurel. *The New Other Woman*. New York: Free Press, 1987.

Ross, Ruth. *Prospering Woman*. San Rafael, California: Whatever Publishing, 1982.

Sanford, Linda, and Mary Ellen Donovan. *Women and Self-Esteem*. New York: Penguin, 1984.

Scarf, Maggie. *Unfinished Business*. New York: Ballantine, 1980.

Sills, Judith. *How to Stop Looking for Someone Perfect and Find Someone to Love*. New York: Ballantine, 1984.

Simon, Barbara Levy. *Never Married Women*. Philadelphia: Temple University Press, 1987.

Storr, Anthony. *Solitude*. New York: Free Press, 1988.

VanCaspel, Vera. *Money Dynamics for the 1990's*. New York: Simon & Schuster, 1989.

Viorst, Judith. *Necessary Losses*. New York: Fawcett, 1986.

———. *How Did I Get to Be 40 and Other Atrocities*. New York: Simon & Schuster, 1973.

Bibliography

Wagner, Jane. *The Search for Signs of Intelligent Life in the Universe.* New York: Harper & Row, 1986.

Weinstein, Grace. *Men, Women and Money.* New York: Signet, 1986.

Woodman, Marian. *Addiction to Perfection.* San Francisco: Inner City Books, 1982.

Working Woman editors, *Working Woman Success Book,* New York: Ace, 1981.

Young-Eisendrath, Polly, and Florence Wiedman. *Female Authority.* New York: Guilford Press, 1987.

Zipes, Jack. *Don't Bet on the Prince.* New York: Methuen, 1986.